INTER ACTIONS

Housing Design in
Uncertain Environments

INTER ACTIONS

Housing Design in
Uncertain Environments

Nadia Charalambous
Giorgos Kyriazis

Acknowledgments

We would like to thank all those whose assistance proved to be essential in the accomplishment of this work. First and foremost, we thank our students at the University of Cyprus, whose work is featured in the second part of this book, "InterFaces." The projects are a small sample of the work conducted during the fourth semester housing studio, an ongoing endeavor to educate future architects in analyzing, understanding, and confronting the complexity of our living environments through design.

We are also grateful to all of those with whom we have had the pleasure to work during the development of this book. We would like to thank the architectural practices who have generously contributed projects which address the book's concerns. Namely, our sincere gratitude to MOS, Urban Nouveau, Ateliermob, and Shigeru Ban for kindly providing their valuable perspectives, project descriptions, and photographs.

The authors would like to thank professionals and communities in Beirut, especially the UN-Habitat Lebanon, who have been part of, or contributed to, the studio's challenges, allowing us to be involved and helping us to develop our ideas.

Finally, we would like to acknowledge with gratitude the support and love of our families; this work would not have been possible without them.

Contents

INTERPRETATIONS

INTERFACES

INTERACTIONS

Preface

This book aims to explore the transformations and uncertainties that shape contemporary living environments. It aspires to unveil critical concerns about the impact of such uncertain practices on the design of living environments, on architectural education, and on the profile of future graduates. It aims at fostering an inquiry into potential responses in the form of policies, design, social innovation, and community initiatives. The above is explored through a reflection on the housing studio pedagogy, aiming, on one hand, to address an apparent gap between the traditional housing studio and the complex, dynamic world, and on the other, to trace and map attempts of housing studio practices to foster and embrace a culture of interActions between the individual student and the team; between different disciplines; between academia, the profession, and the community; and between global driving forces and local contexts.

INTRODUCTION

Understanding the ways in which the home as a spatial form relates to the social, the cultural, and the individual in the context of the increasingly divided, complex, uncertain, and differentiated experiences of contemporary life is one of the central challenges addressed in this book. Having, as a starting point, the complexity of factors that have shaped living environments in cities though time, the book seeks to explore, understand, and map uncertainties that shape contemporary urban living, and housing in particular, in a critical manner; unveil critical concerns on the impact of such unsettling practices on the design and production of living environments; foster and embrace a culture of interFaces between the individual student and the team, between different disciplines, between academia, the community, and the profession, and between global driving forces and local contexts in order to proactively address, adapt, and respond to change.

Reflecting on the above, the book is structured in three interrelated sections:

InterPretations: Emerging themes in contemporary housing research and housing design education are reviewed. This section is dedicated to mapping the relevant field of research, discussing contemporary housing challenges in uncertain geographies, and identifying relevant issues and themes.

InterFaces: Housing studio pedagogy that attempts to understand and address uncertainties that shape contemporary urban living are explored in this section. Conditions of the unsettled and the respective challenges posed to the design of housing are discussed through a reflection on socially-engaged, design studio experiences.

InterActions: Housing projects developed by international architectural practices that aim to embrace a culture of interActions through complex collaborative processes, involving a number of actors representing a vast range of knowledge, experiences, and agendas are presented. This section is dedicated to illustrating, through case studies from architectural practice, some of the subjects addressed in the book such as community participation and collaborative practices.

The book addresses academics, practitioners, graduate students, and professional associations that make decisions about education. Aiming at a pedagogical dialogue on architecture and housing design it resets the stage for debating future visions of housing studio pedagogy. While capturing the body of knowledge required for seeking this new form of pedagogy, the book introduces student-centered educational processes based on actual experiences that could ultimately transform this knowledge into guiding pedagogical principles and teaching practices toward a more responsive pedagogy in housing design.

InterPretations. The gap between the reality of a changing world and the established teaching and learning models is addressed in the first section of the book, "Responding to Uncertainty through the Housing Design Studio Pedagogy: Implications and Opportunities for Architectural Education."

This part identifies the fast, and often abrupt, transformations of contemporary living environments and housing around the world as a result of multiple forces: globalization, increased mobility at all levels, massive internal movements of labor, technological developments, and economic fluctuations, among others. These changes have resulted in conditions of uncertainty and increasingly complex challenges such as the lack of affordable housing, overcrowding, dislocation of population due to gentrification, natural and/or other disasters, sociospatial inequalities, and social integration problems.

These ubiquitous and tangible transformations affecting our living environments entail a respective transformation of architectural practice and challenge the architects' ability to handle such complexity. This has direct implications on architectural education and on the profile of future graduates. Design studio culture and pedagogy need to be reviewed to proactively address these global changes in order to prepare architects to be able to effectively deal with complex, multi-layered, and uncertain living environments.

However, a gap between the reality of a changing world and the established teaching and learning models of the design studio is identified. Architectural education—in particular the housing design studio pedagogy—seems to be an isolated island in the middle of a complex reality. The need to overcome the insularity of the housing studio stems from the aspirations of the users and society at large, as well as from the need to bring the architectural profession up to date. To overcome this insularity, housing design education needs to explore how designers can acquire a deeper understanding of the conditions of uncertainty and unsettledness that are prevalent in many parts of the larger socioeconomic processes that have an impact on cities and on the different groups inhabiting our living environments.

The argument for a public-spirited, evidence-based education is advanced; this implies a pedagogical approach that makes research, student learning, and external engagement relate to societal needs and aspirations. The housing design studio is a fertile ground where this can happen, since it marks the passage from the description, understanding, and explanation of cities and our living environments to the act of producing new urban forms in the educational environment.

A number of key issues concerning the transformation of our living environments and architectural education in the globalized society are explored in this section, in an attempt to map and address the apparent gap between the traditional housing studio and the complex, dynamic world. The topics discussed include multidisciplinary approaches in studio pedagogy, going beyond disciplinary and academic boundaries, and canceling out the tensions between global dynamics, cultural diversity, and local realities.

The chapter concludes with the identification of the need for housing studio practices to embrace a culture of interFaces between the individual student and the team; between different disciplines; between academia, the profession and the community; and between global driving forces and local contexts.

InterFaces. The considerations that are presented in the first part of the book translate naturally into the educational setting and above all to the design studio; the latter is still considered as the backbone of architectural education, the passage from the description, understanding, and explanation of cities to the act of producing new urban forms in the educational environment.

Situated within an educational framework that is culturally grounded and focused in the real world, the studio AtHome, currently taught at the University of Cyprus, aims to develop processes, knowledge, and skills that will enable housing actors to contribute to sustainable, just, and socially inclusive living environments, in order to proactively address, adapt, and respond to change and uncertainty.

Contributing to positive change requires deep awareness of the wider context of living environments but also of the immediate context in which change is to be implemented. A thorough understanding and interpretation of the relevant field of research, the discussion of contemporary housing challenges in uncertain geographies, and the critical identification of relevant issues and themes is an essential first step to better understand the wider context. Traditional concepts of the dwelling are challenged and questioned; the experience of urban life in the twenty-first century—transient, fragmented, changeable, and unpredictable—contrasts to concepts of dwelling based on stability, permanence, locality, and a sense of belonging.

Within this framework, a discussion on the global dimension of housing in contemporary societies evolves based on the existence of common driving forces influencing the contemporary habitat in different cultures, societies, and places, including: sociodemographic changes and transformed family structures, intense mobility and dislocated publics (migration, refugees), affordability, and access to housing. Without denying the existence of global forces that push towards the aforementioned changes, students are encouraged to understand that in cities around the world such changes are related to the specific shape of local sociospatial realities, acknowledging the increased tensions between global forces and local cultures and specificities.

An in-depth, hands-on understanding of the actual context/site is then encouraged. Central to the studio's methodology is an action-research, process-oriented, and evidence-based approach that focuses on issues defined by a nuanced understanding of the immediate context. By "immediate context" the studio refers to the specific intertwining of three major spheres: (1) the economic and political spheres and the implications on housing policies, affordability, and access; (2) the social sphere, which includes social and family networks, everyday practices, institutions, and other local organizations; as well as the wide network of agents directly or indirectly involved in the shaping of the built environment, both locally and globally. "Context" also extends to (3) the specific and durable shape of local sociospatial realities, i.e. the physical form of the built environment, social relations inscribed in spatial patterns, urban histories and ideologies, and environmental conditions.

The projects presented address the studio's objectives in different ways, raising questions about design education in an international context; post-conflict rehabilitation of dislocated publics and vulnerable groups; affordable housing through social entrepreneurship, shared activities and spaces, and redefined family networks.

InterActions. The last section fosters an inquiry into potential responses to contemporary conditions of uncertainty in the form of professional practice, design, social innovation, and/or community initiatives. Housing projects developed by four architectural practices that aim to embrace a culture of interActions through complex collaborative processes, involving a number of actors representing a vast range of knowledge, experiences, and agendas are presented and discussed. The presentation of the case studies is underpinned, though not limited by, some general guiding questions that aim to reflect on the ways that changes and transformations of living environments have affected architectural practice; the emergence of new forms of architectural practices, collaborations, and multi-disciplinary approaches, participatory practices, and contemporary definitions of the "context."

The professional practices of MOS, Ateliermob, Urban Nouveau, and Shigeru Ban as well as the work undertaken by UN-Habitat in Lebanon present a new body of work that it is influenced by the new order of things such as the financial and environmental crisis, sociopolitical instabilities, and increased mobility. Alternative modes of practicing reveal new forms of operation in transformed contexts and for users not previously confronted.

As part of its program on "Enhancing the Role of Unions of Municipalities to Respond to Refugees' and Host Communities' Needs" funded by UNICEF, **UN-Habitat in Lebanon** has organized extensive awareness-raising campaigns and activities that to date have targeted 7,336 refugees and 7,936 people from the host population with the overall aim to reduce health problems through behavioral changes and to address urban issues, including access to housing and neighborhood public spaces.

All UN-Habitat projects are learning opportunities as cities and neighborhoods in Lebanon are constantly in flux, and security and access always remain an issue. Every project is an opportunity to learn and bring in new partners from national and local governments, agencies, academia, or the private sector, which always contributes to the successful implementation of the project by bringing in new capabilities and perspectives to work together towards building a better urban future in Lebanon. The project presented describes the process of implementing a safe, inclusive, and accessible public space in Naba'a, a low-income neighborhood in eastern Beirut, through the participation and training of the local community.

Michael Meredith and Hilary Sample are American architects and co-founders of the award-winning architecture firm **MOS** Architects in New York City. Meredith and Sample teach at Princeton University School of Architecture and Columbia University, respectively, and their academic research and teaching occurs in parallel to the real-world constraints of practice, informing both. Recent projects include four studio buildings for the Krabbesholm Højskole campus and the Apan Housing Laboratory. Tasked with accepting large groups bused to the site, the Apan project addresses the diversity of users and uses, as well as the need for low-cost housing, through proposing different housing prototypes, educating students, and providing short-term workspace.

The birth of **Urban Nouveau** took place in India during the realization of their first project, Incremental India. The architects were deeply concerned with the fact that in spite of great progress in improving urban villages and preventing their formation, this challenge remains a critical factor for the persistence of poverty in the world. These concerns fueled the architects' interest in proposing affordable social housing, developed in close collaboration with the existing inhabitants and local stakeholders. Despite the fact that the whole process was fraught with difficulties, it is underpinned by valuable insights, tools, and methodologies in addressing inequalities, exclusion, and lack of accessibility to basic housing needs, through a nuanced understanding and mapping of the context as well as through collaborative practices throughout the design process.

Shigeru Ban is well known for his humanitarian approach to design, which addresses the needs of displaced populations as a result of natural disasters. This particular work addresses timely challenges faced by contemporary architects such as the absence of the "traditional" client and the need for social entrepreneurship, for social responsibility, and a nuanced understanding of the local context and the people's cultural and social makeup. For the past three decades, Shigeru Ban has applied his extensive knowledge of recyclable, inexpensive local materials, particularly paper and cardboard, to constructing high-quality, low-cost shelters for victims of disaster across the world, training and involving local resources and labor in the process.

Ateliermob, a company founded in 2005 in Lisbon, is a multidisciplinary platform for the development of ideas, research, and projects in the areas of architecture, landscape, design, and urbanism. In 2016, the cooperative Working with the 99% was created for the provision of services in the fields of architecture and social or intervention design, urban planning, strategic planning, coordination and implementation of projects, and training. Tiago Mota Saraiva, one of the company's partners, highlights key issues through an interview, including among others the need for a broader understanding of the housing contexts, crowdsourcing and funding initiatives through a better understanding of the contemporary "client," and socially responsible architecture. He argues in favor of some principles that are foundational to the company when discussing housing matters: the right to housing, to basic energy supply, to the city, and to place.

INTER

Living environments and housing around the world have become transformed in the past few decades as a result of multiple forces: globalization, massive internal movements of labor, technological developments, and economic fluctuations, among others. These changes have resulted in conditions of uncertainty and increasingly complex challenges such as the lack of affordable housing, overcrowding, dislocation of population, gentrification, natural and other disasters, and sociospatial inequalities.

These ubiquitous and tangible transformations affecting our living environments challenge the architects' ability to handle such complexity. This has direct implications on architectural education and on the profile of future graduates. Design studio culture and pedagogy need to be reviewed to proactively address these global changes in order to prepare architects to be able to effectively deal with complex, multi-layered, cross-cultural, and uncertain living environments.

However, a gap between the reality of a changing world and the established teaching and learning models of the design studio is identified. Architectural education—in particular the housing design studio pedagogy—seems in some cases to be an isolated island

PRETATIONS

in the middle of a complex reality. To overcome this insularity, housing design education needs to explore how designers can acquire a deeper understanding of the conditions of uncertainty and unsettledness that have an impact on cities and on the different groups inhabiting our living environments.

The housing design studio is a fertile ground where this can happen, since it marks the passage from the description, understanding, and explanation of cities to the act of producing new urban forms. An environment that nurtures exploration and critical thinking needs to be fostered. This section discusses the integration of experiential learning, through action-research, into teaching by arguing for the exposure of students to primary source materials that enable them to get as close as possible to the realities being studied.

A number of key issues are explored in an attempt to map and address the apparent gap between the traditional housing studio and the complexity of the realities beyond academia. The topics discussed include evidence-based housing design, multidisciplinary approaches in studio pedagogy, and live projects beyond the academic environment.

Responding to Uncertainty through the Housing Design Studio Pedagogy: Implications and Opportunities for Architectural Education

Nadia Charalambous

Global Patterns, Social Change, and Transformation of Living Environments

Living environments are complex entities that are constantly changing in terms of demography, social structures, and spatial arrangements. Over the past few decades, cities around the world have become radically altered in the sense of scale, scope, and complexity as a result of globalization, increased mobility at all levels, climate and technological change, migration as well as internal displacements and the movement of refugees, changes in social structures, privatization, labor market instability, gentrification, and real estate market tensions (Marcuse & Van Kempen, 2000). These ubiquitous changes entailed the creation of a diverse urban population and a respective transformation of living environments, where the everyday life of the diverse groups living in cities unfolds. Demographic, spatial, and sociocultural changes have had a direct impact on everyday patterns of living, domestic activities, and family structures (Fokkema & Liefbroer, 2008).

Discussions on social inequalities, urban segregation, social justice, and the right to the city as well as a strong critique of unfair urban patterns have become prominent, fueling debates over power relations in times of rapid urban and societal transformations, uncertainty, and crisis. Unequal access to housing, affordability, homelessness, overcrowding, and social integration—the goals of the 2030 Agenda for Sustainable Development and the UN Conference on Housing and Sustainable Urban Development—are discussed in the context of dynamic urban growth. Questions of inclusion, access, and opportunity have been negotiated in the context of globalization, changing forms of production, declining welfare, and developing technologies. The current debate on the global dimension of housing highlights the uncertainty that characterizes all aspects of contemporary living in many parts of the world; issues such as access to housing, affordability, sustainability, and participation in the creation of living environments have become prominent.

Societal trends such as accelerating urbanization have reduced the availability of affordable housing worldwide. Once considered an obligation of the welfare state, housing has become an asset and a service to be acquired in the free market, which not everybody can afford. As the welfare state has diminished and housing supply has been taken over by the private sector, the lack of affordable housing has become an endemic problem, particularly in major cities where job opportunities are concentrated. The most vulnerable segments of the population (single parents, homeless, young and elderly) are not the only people who have difficulty accessing housing. Nowadays, the supply of quality housing represents a global challenge illustrated by acute shortages and affordability issues. Problems with homelessness, overcrowding, tenure security, substandard housing, and segregation and clustering of poor quality housing are challenging problems in many countries. Lack of affordable and accessible housing creates numerous socioeconomic problems, such as inadequate housing conditions, the emergence and expansion of slum and informal settlement areas, homelessness, and unsustainable commuting patterns.

The disappearance of support for social housing has led to a huge need for new housing design solutions and innovative procurement models. The adoption of new roles by citizens, professionals, the private sector, and public bodies, who have each a shared role in the development of solutions, is urgently needed. The provision of affordable housing is a cross-cutting issue involving architecture, construction, community, finance, and policies. Innovative design solutions, financial models, procurement methods, governance structures, and cross-cutting practice models are explored to engage the various sectors in the provision of affordable housing.

Affordability in contemporary housing is not simply a financial issue, but a more complex question of how the society at large can embed housing demands into everyday architecture. Access to decent affordable housing is a fundamental determinant of people's welfare, and it plays an important role in strengthening social integration and social cohesion. At a global level, the resilient cities debate addresses affordability through a focus on the physical, social, and economic challenges faced nowadays by cities. Affordable housing to facilitate sustainable cities for all is a significant global challenge as acknowledged by the UN-Habitat and the Global Network for Sustainable Housing.

Public sensibility about sustainable development is on the increase as citizens and communities are aware of the benefit of its effect on their well-being and to the common good. Sustainability encompasses the intertwined areas of environmental protection, economic growth, and social development. With reference to housing, it embraces the building, city, and regional scales; physical structures (at the building and urban level) and social structures; newly built housing and the retrofitting of the existing building stock. At the same time, there is a steadily increasing gap between existing housing stock and resident needs: today's social structures (more diverse and less stable) and lifestyles (more mobile and versatile) demand new kind of flexible and adaptable homes. Sustainable housing design should also be responsive to demographic change and sensitive to new and emerging living arrangements. Large-scale renovation programs, strongly knitted with strategies to improve entrepreneurialism, skills development, and training in order to improve the economy at a local level, are needed to respond to these changes. Such social-oriented housing programs need to be supported by appropriate policies, carried out by established organizations with secure funding, and with the support of local administrations and communities.

UN-Habitat highlights the importance of empowering and engaging citizens in the shaping of their living environments to ensure a sustainable development and to contribute to promoting a sense of community by bringing together people who share common goals and facilitating what is referred to as collective intelligence (Fischer, Giaccardi, Eden, Sugimoto, & Ye, 2005). Advocates of such an approach argue that a more democratic participation may raise awareness of the cultural and social qualities of localities at the policy-making stage, and consequently avoid conflicts that might later require greater policy implementation.[1] Several scholars suggest that the active engagement of citizens—from the early planning stages to the operation and use—will foster social cohesion and affordability and will engage different groups in the process of urban and housing development while also measuring the impact of new interventions and regeneration strategies on housing growth and the continuously changing needs of local communities.[2]

On the other hand, some opponents to participatory processes contend that they produce consensus through the digestion or dilution of conflicts, thus preventing the system from changing and resulting in homogeneity (Miessen, 2011). Community participation in the context of housing delivery, as in any other context, runs the risk of becoming an empty ritual, which allows the power-holders to claim that all sides have been considered, without any real redistribution of power. In this regard, Cooke and Kothari (2001) have argued that participatory processes are just marketing tools for "outsiders" to legitimize interventions. Opposing this view, Hickey and Mohan (2004, 3) among others, considered participation to be a "legitimate and genuinely transformative approach to development."

The aforementioned brief literature review reveals that a transformed living environment is the result of the rapid changes, increased tensions between global forces and local realities, cultural diversity, and the involvement of a large number of agents and stakeholders. The need to address contemporary living environments collaboratively, through a multidimensional, cross-sectoral perspective encompassing all the factors which condition the various forms of dwelling in today's societies—architectural, urban, environmental, economic, political, cultural, and social—emerges, and leads to an enormous increase in the complexity of the issues, which housing actors in general and architects in particular, have to deal with. Furthermore, it is necessary to consider the ongoing transformations affecting multiple scales and realms, from the level of the housing unit to the building and to the city; from the physical to the social

1 The concept of community or citizen participation has been open to various interpretations as well as a degree of misuse. Participatory design builds on the ideals of a participatory democracy, where collective decision-making is highly decentralized throughout all sectors of society, so that all individuals can effectively participate in taking decisions that affect them in their daily environment (Sanoff, 2011). Participatory design practitioners might vary with regard to their perspectives, backgrounds, and interests. However, they all share the view that design ideas arise in collaboration and that every participant is an expert in what they do. Therefore, it is important for all parties concerned to listen to each other's views and to work effectively as a multidisciplinary team. In this way everyone's opinion is considered and integrated into the final design.

2 Community participation can create a sense of ownership, which in turn can increase subsequent prospects for the adequate maintenance of the housing stock. In certain contexts, especially in developing countries, training community members in sustainable construction techniques can help them to acquire marketable skills, which in turn leads to an increase in social capital and to improvements in local economic development. In post-crisis contexts, early intervention recovery is the right time to initiate participatory processes to guide reconstruction and provide durable and sustainable housing solutions.

structures; and from global driving forces to local economic, social and urban environments. It becomes necessary to face an endemic lack of sustainable and affordable housing from new perspectives in order to understand all the dimensions (architectural, urban, social, economic, political, environmental, governance) involved and their multiple interrelationships.

The aforementioned discussion challenges the role and ability of urban designers, architects, and public urban design and planning institutions in responding to contemporary housing transformations in the midst of uncertain conditions. This stance leads to the question whether architecture, urban design, and planning institutions can not only acknowledge these transformations and the conditions of uncertainty surrounding our living environments but also provide helpful, just, and concord-based ways to address it. This paper proposes that the answer is positive. It is suggested that to do so requires architects, planners, and urban designers to cast a spatial lens on uncertainty, learn from unsettled activities, and respond through humbler and more nuanced design thinking, processes, and spatial practices than those conventionally taught and practiced.

A holistic, multidisciplinary investigation into contemporary housing is necessary to create the tools, methods, and policies that can then be implemented—by adequately trained architects and planners, by informed industrial and community stakeholders, and by innovative investors—to properly address the challenge of contemporary housing. This includes a review of current learning and teaching programs in architecture and urban planning schools at all levels in order to train future graduates to have the capacity to implement solutions that help to achieve sustainable development goals. Emerging concerns about undergraduate pedagogy present new opportunities for us as academics to strengthen our programs, to enhance our role in shaping education, and to improve the quality of that education.

Implications and Opportunities for Architectural Education
A first step towards achieving this goal is to reflect on the educa-

tion of the future shapers of living environments. The process of educating future architects and designers around the world varies dramatically. However, despite the considerable differences in the content, structure, and delivery of architectural and urban education, there is one remarkable similarity: the overriding primacy given to the design studio as the main forum of creative exploration, interAction, and assimilation. Unlike other disciplinary teaching, the design studio is conceived as a complex overlapping of learning, practice, making, and thinking, all happening in this special place, the studio. Ashraf Salama (2008) describes the design studio as a pedagogy that conserves and transmits the values of design professions and society at large. As such, appropriate design studios are necessary to help train future housing actors in this endeavor, particularly in re-envisioning a renewed approach needed to effectively and efficiently address contemporary housing conditions.

A number of studies argue that any ongoing changes in the design studio are not aligned with today's rapidly changing world (Koch, Shwennsen, Dutton, & Smith, 2002; Tzonis, 2014).[3] Through it all, the cultural values and practices underpinning architecture studios seem to have largely withstood change. According to a report prepared by the American Institute of Architecture Students (AIAS), contemporary studio pedagogy cannot effectively cope with the changing nature of the built environment or the transformations undergone in architectural practice (Koch et al., 2002). In many cases, architectural educators continue designing and teaching the studio on the basis of what an architect currently is or was, with the aim of developing individual skills and critical thinking abilities that do not seem to respond to the transformed and expanded demands placed on the profession by society.

Design studios have drawn a number of critical appreciations over the years. One of the earlier critics was Donald Schön (1984), who nevertheless perceived studios as unsurpassed in their potential for teaching future professionals through learning-by-doing and "reflection-in-action." Kathryn Antony (1991, 167) found the design studio's tendency to train the designer as a solo artist inconsistent

3 These concerns are not new. They have emerged in one form or another, from early reform efforts by John Dewey, Alfred Whitehead, and Jean Piaget, to the experimental colleges of the 1960s and the work of Benjamin Bloom and more recently David Kolb. However, in the last few years, the level of concern has intensified.

4 One needs to mention the important pedagogical experiments that played a crucial role in shaping architectural discourse and practice in the second half of the twentieth century. According to Colomina, Choi, Galan, and Meister (2012), these radical practices paved the way to a new modus operandi for the discipline, which could only be created if "traditions were questioned, destabilized, undermined or even destroyed." In the US, since the civil rights movement of the 1960s, there has also been a growing emphasis on service learning studios in rural communities and inner-city neighborhoods (Anthony, 2011) such as the University of Auburn's Rural Studio, founded in 1992 in Hale, Alabama, by Professor Samuel Mockbee. While architecture studios, often focused on specific design projects, have led this approach (Boyer and Mitgang 1996), several urban design and planning studios have followed a model of civic engagement and community service (Hardin, Eribes, and Poster 2006). In the wake of Hurricane Katrina in New Orleans, several urban design and planning programs organized studio opportunities for their students (Antony, 2011).

5 At its best, studio pedagogy has many strengths: it can promote and support critical, analytic, and synthetic thinking through the exploration of the relationship between design and the cultural context, and it can convey, transmit, or even transform the values of the design profession and society at large. At its worst, it may facilitate isolation from the real world, conserving, sustaining, and reproducing existing preconcep-

with "the increasingly complex nature of the professional world." Leon van Schaik (2008, 84) expressed a similar concern a while ago, when claiming that:

architecture has no real connection to the daily expectations of citizens, but it is seen rather as a brutal instrumental servant to corporate or governmental interests; or as a purveyance of esoteric spatial luxuries to domestic elites. In the Anglophone world for example, for the last few decades, statistics reveal that architects design less than eight per cent of houses and housing.

So, despite the dynamic and ubiquitous changes taking place in our time, respective changes in architectural education and studio pedagogy have been rare, apart from minor attempts to reconfigure the structure of studio content and to rethink the way in which knowledge is delivered and experienced in response to a changing world (Tzonis, 2014).[4] According to Salama, the diversity of issues and the lack of common understanding are resulting in a lack of consensus among educators and academics on the issue of what changes and developments in architectural and urban pedagogy will best meet the needs of design professions while supporting the aspirations of contemporary societies (Salama, 2008). Tzonis (2014), on the other hand, points out that the challenge that architectural education faces today is not to enrich and adapt the core knowledge to the changing world, but to reformulate the studio framework itself.

Within this framework, Dorst (2008) suggests that we need to rethink the object of the architecture studio as well as the very nature of the tools and methods studio education needs to create in order to meet current challenges. The studio structure has its own culture, patterns, and values that are passed on over the years, through generations of students, educators, and practitioners and are highly influential in a student's education and future practice (Dutton, 1991).[5] A prevalent pedagogic approach in the studio that remains detached from the reality of the built environment does not help to overcome the gap between academic education and the dynamic and complex world.[6] Studio culture and pedagogy need to be questioned and revised to proactively address changes and to produce engaging and well-formed graduate architects who are able to deal effectively with a complex, multi-layered, and uncertain built environment and profession (Koch et al., 2002).

Salama (2008), discussing architectural education in most of the "Western" world, points to deficiencies in architectural education, particularly in areas of theory and knowledge building, without which, he claims, the value of the architectural services cannot be properly articulated. Thus, architecture's contribution to and engagement with society is made difficult. He argues that without research, scholarship, and a rigorous knowledge base, the profession cannot take stands on significant health, economic, social, political, and ethical issues that we face in the world. An approach for a more effective integration of research and design activities is proposed, to effectively utilize knowledge and information that are derived from everyday life and social needs and concerns. Encompassing a wide spectrum of techniques that are student-centered, process-oriented, and knowledge-based, the ultimate objective according to Salama (2008), is to invigorate an evidence-based culture in design studio teaching practices.

The argument for a public-spirited, evidence-based education is advanced. A public-spirited education at its best implies the need to engage with what is often termed the "*real world*"; to engage with society and its political and economic processes, among others (Cossio M.B. 2011). It also implies a pedagogical approach that makes research, student learning, and external engagement relate to societal needs and aspirations. This necessitates a systematic rational and empirical engagement with the real world, addressing pressing societal problems in research, producing graduates prepared for responsibility, and promoting inquiry and open debate based on evidence and reason.

John Habraken identifies three missing aspects in the design studio, or "Three Points of Conflict," which keep us disengaged with "everyday environment". These elements are: *change,* to keep up

tions and stereotypes and resisting change (Dutton, 1991).

6 Students in Europe and the US were trained and socialized in the conventional emphasis and strategies of housing design (Antony, 2011). In such cases, even if the studio's sites were real, students were not asked to spend time there, observe and understand ongoing social activities, or interact with users. Even today, the great bulk of activities in typical design studios take place in the classroom—from the computer-aided mapping of the site's urban fabric to the final presentation of design interventions in front of a "jury of experts"—detaching students from the existing socioeconomic and cultural factors that should determine the transformation of a site.

7 The discussion of reality or the 'real world' does not stem from a philosophical perspective. The term 'reality' is referred to as the ordinary, the everyday experience of the real world. The *real world*, the *world out there*, reflects the 'wider community' and society's most urgent needs.

with social, technological, and urban changes; *control*, in the form of "distributed design control," which "renders large projects fine grained and sustainable"; and *values*, including the value of *sharing* which challenges individualistic expressions of architecture (Habraken, 2007, 14). He points to the need for balancing the creative act required for successful design and the social and environmental responsibilities that should be embedded in this act.

Not all educators will agree with the need to scrutinize the design studio from a point of view of its engagement with the real world. Counter arguments note that there are advantages offered by "imaginary" themes that "real" situations do not provide and referred to this particular condition within the design studio as, "*a virtual world that represents the real world of practice but it is relatively free of its pressures, distractions and risks*" (Schon, 1988, 5). Some, while sharing similar concerns regarding architecture's disconnection with the real world, may not share the view that the answer, or part of the answer, can be found in architectural education. Arguments against emulating the reality of practice in the design studio believe that it may diminish the opportunity of creative freedom (Cossio, 2011).

In line with Cossio's (2011) argument, this paper posits that "creative freedom" in the design studio should not be conditioned by disengagement; it should rather be fostered by *experience, knowledge, reason, and judgment*, qualities that can be attained by engaging with the real world. New demands challenge our everyday life and they are manifested in sociospatial changes to our cities. It is in this wider context that the relatively minor aspirations of architectural education justify scrutiny in relation to their relevance and practicability. The need for a type of education that recognizes the changes taking place in society and is able to consciously take part and contribute to these changes is evident. In these critical times, the influential power of education can assist to steer positive change. As Henry Sanoff suggests (2007, 21):

The quality of life can be improved by improving the quality of our education and the environment—both in crisis—the need for an interac-

tive human/environment learning system has never been more pressing than today.

At an international level, the Union of International Architects (UIA, 2005) has tried to address current global concerns, including environmental issues, through its educational charter, highlighting the architect's social responsibility, stating:

Beyond all aesthetic, technical and financial aspects of the professional responsibilities, the major concerns, expressed by the Charter, are the social commitment of the profession, i.e. the awareness of the role and responsibility of the architect in his or her respective society, as well as the improvement of the quality of life through sustainable human settlements.

Implied in the above is the notion that awareness and engagement with the social, political, environmental, and economic realities ensures the legitimacy of the profession and with it, its capacity to influence change; a pledge to public interest and social responsibility is made. Understanding architectural education and its relationship with the real world becomes crucial if we are to assess its current condition and, more importantly, if we are to plan for the future of that education. Conflicting desires, aspirations, needs, and commercial realities of all stakeholders involved in the design process create intense tensions in architectural education but also present new opportunities. This paper argues that housing design should be concerned and has indeed a great deal to offer in addressing and responding to the needs and particular circumstances of specific population segments that are the primary actors in contemporary living environments by providing future architects with the skills to efficiently and humanly respond to ordinary life needs. Perhaps the recent, renewed interest for live studios and socially engaged design studio pedagogy are expressions of these concerns, stating that *corporatism* and *consumerism* are not the only reality within which the design studio can operate, nor its only horizon.

Within this context, the paper posits that designers need to take notice of the conditions of uncertainty in its grounded context in

8 Boyer and Mitgang (1996) expressed such concerns in the 1990s, pointing out a disconnection of the design studio from society as well as a sense of social, physical, and intellectual isolation of architecture schools on their own campuses. As Anthony (1991) pointed out, the studio has gradually acquired such a central role in students' social lives that it has reduced the importance of the world outside.

order to better understand and positively intervene in uncertain urban landscapes. For this to happen, housing design education should focus on how designers can acquire a deeper understanding of the larger socioeconomic processes that have an impact on urban form and on the different groups inhabiting our living environments. The housing design studio is a fertile ground where this can happen, since it marks the passage from the description, understanding, and explanation of cities and our living environments to the act of producing new urban forms in the educational environment. It can provide an excellent opportunity for students to understand uncertainty and unsettledness but also to appreciate the limits of design-based approaches in addressing complex issues.

The following part of the paper reflects on the potential to revisit the nature of the link between the housing design studio content and the so-called outside-world. An attempt to address the apparent gap between the traditional housing studio and the complex, dynamic world involves dealing with a number of relevant topics such as multidisciplinary approaches in studio pedagogy, going beyond disciplinary and academic boundaries, and canceling out the tensions between global dynamics, cultural diversity, and local realities.

A framework of responding to uncertainty through housing design is articulated, focusing on interPretation of the scope and context, facilitating interFaces between the different actors/agents involved, and embracing a culture of interActions.

Addressing Uncertainty through the Housing Design Studio: Locating Learning between Academia and the Everyday

The need to address the insularity of the housing studio and the architecture student from the needs and goals of the users and the society at large, as well as from advances in the profession itself, has emerged from the above discussions.[8] A call for change in all these studies indicates a general agreement on the need for the reorientation of the housing studio education towards an engaging approach that also considers the social responsibility of future architects. The need to instill a sense of involvement in the students emerges. This involvement refers not only to the community they will eventually serve but also to their future professional activity, drawing on knowledge that supersedes the disciplinary boundaries and the academic limits and draws on all agents/stakeholders involved.

InterPretations

Contributing to positive change requires deep awareness of the context of the environment in which change is to be implemented. A thorough understanding and interpretation of the relevant field of research, the discussion of contemporary housing challenges in uncertain geographies, and the critical identification of relevant issues and themes are essential first steps to better understand the context. By context we refer to the specific intertwining of three major spheres: (1) the economic and political spheres and their implications on housing policies, affordability, and access; (2) the social sphere that includes social and family networks, everyday practices, institutions and other local organizations as well as the wide network of agents directly or indirectly involved in the shaping of the built environment, both locally and globally; context also extends to (3) the specific and durable shape of local sociospatial realities, i.e. the physical form of the built environment, social relations inscribed in spatial patterns, urban histories and ideologies, and environmental conditions.

This approach can address a serious challenge that the housing studio faces today in training future housing actors to deal effectively with the increased tensions between global forces and distinct local sociospatial realities. On one hand, traditional concepts of housing in general and the dwelling in particular, as well as the identification of dwelling with a permanent place of residence and a specific context are being increasingly questioned. The experience of urban life in the twenty-first century—transient, fragmented, changeable, and uncertain—contrasts to concepts of dwelling based on stability, permanence, locality, and a sense of belonging. Theorists point out that the demands of mobility, the vast number of possible choices, and massive waves of refugees—resulting from political decisions such as the unification of Europe—have undermined our inclination and abilities to form ties with a place (Lefas, 2009).

However, without denying the existence and the importance of global driving forces, researchers have also illustrated that in cities around the world there are often alternative local contingencies that contrast with the globalized, abstract theoretical approaches (Maloutas & Fujita, 2012). Although houses everywhere serve the same basic needs and activities, a glance at the architectural record reveals an astonishing variety in the ways in which these activities are accommodated in the houses of different cultures and places (Hanson, 1998). Cultural diversity and the significant differences observed in housing around the globe highlight the inherent complexity and context-bound nature of everyday environments that are also strongly related to the specific local sociospatial realities. Conditions of uncertainty may be particularly complex with multiple stakeholders and involve the potential for conflict among different groups. Responding to uncertainty requires considering and understanding the particular sociospatial circumstances, cultural specificities, power dynamics, economic potentials, and imperatives of different informal activities and their actors in different city contexts before deciding on a design action or strategy.

The latter calls for educating future practitioners to serve local communities by drawing on essential local knowledge, which needs to be taken into account in architectural education (Lefaivre & Tzonis, 2012). The ability to deal effectively with such tensions relates to fostering appropriate design-thinking skills, which will facilitate students' ability to design housing, taking into account the potentials and constraints of a particular context. The need to address contemporary living environments through a multidimensional, cross-sectoral perspective encompassing all the factors that condition the various forms of dwelling in today's societies—architectural, urban, environmental, economic, political, cultural, and social—emerges, and leads to an enormous increase in the complexity of the issues that housing actors in general and architects in particular have to deal with. Rather than multiple perspectives of reality, it is in a merging of multiple aspects—within their context, their complex, their totality—an intersection rather than a selection between the multiple educational concerns or perspectives, where real learning occurs. The need to foster a fruitful, open, dialogue through facilitating interFaces between all factors involved is evident.

InterFaces

Disciplinary interFaces. In order to address the above, the housing design studio needs to stake its claims amid a new territory by articulating its relationship with the technological, sociopolitical, and cultural transformations of the time. The current conception of housing design needs to move towards a discourse that uncovers latent possibilities within the complex and fluid interaction of a number of factors with the participation of a growing number of agents and stakeholders in the creation of living environments. New types of interdisciplinary knowledge arising from all these driving forces in different realms (sociological, political, economic, environmental, ecological, among others) are needed to make informed design decisions in order to enable a reevaluation of the way we create, preserve, and alter living environments in our time.

The housing studio can then provide opportunities for an integrated approach from the early stages of the design process to explore the multidimensionality of living environments and thus to facilitate the merging of inputs coming through research, the profession, and the community. It can be reevaluated to assess whether students are indeed exposed to the complex set of issues that they will be asked to address once they graduate.[9] Accordingly, one challenge confronting housing studio educators is to facilitate interFaces both within the curriculum and the individual students (through collaborative practices) and between the housing studio and other disciplines on campus.

InterFaces between academia and the real world. A further concern is the lack of involvement of architecture students in their own communities, acknowledging the important role that local contexts, clients, and users play in the housing design process. The

9 For instance, a major challenge that the housing studio faces today is to expose students to the knowledge required to deal with rapid and complex demographic and sociocultural changes that have a direct impact on everyday patterns of living, family structures, and living arrangements. (Billari, Kohler, Andersson, & Lundström, 2007; Bongaarts, 2006). The consequences of these changes in living arrangements and household types in different contexts are discussed in numerous sociological, economic and other studies, and need to inform the housing studio in order to facilitate a more nuanced understanding of housing contexts in the real world.

10 Live project work can be seen as located between the academy and the everyday. Students test out their learning in practice, acting professionally, but still working in the role of students, locating their work outside in the community, while also benefiting from the support of the university. Through locating the projects outside of the classroom but providing space for the critical reflection that we promote within the classroom, students are given the opportunity to critique and reenergize traditional modes of practice, in the *modi operandi* of their education and their profession.

housing studio needs to be concerned with the responsibility of future architects towards society and community service, with the social and cultural implications of designing for the society. Hou and Kinoshita (2007, 310) argue that informal processes in design (neighborhood events, walking tours, meals, and informal convenings and conversations) can at times overcome the limitations of formal participatory processes, which may not (or should not) be possible in the educational environment as they "*produce new meanings, relationships, and collective actions that allow community actors to overcome formal barriers and social and cultural differences.*" Such informal processes can also be useful for students in housing design studios, encouraging a revised practice of housing design. The seeds for such a practice should be first planted in the classroom and integrated in the training of housing design students by building awareness of potential interFaces as a first step paving the way for meaningful interaction.

InterActions

InterActing with the community. Carrying out these strategies with the involvement of the affected communities requires future graduates to become exposed to the potential to work as mediators, to understand building and urban transformation processes with the participation of residents, skills that are not acquired in the planning and architecture schools. Bridging the gaps through meaningful and constructive interaction with both the community and the profession through live projects should be a major objective of housing design studio educators.[10] Students can gain valuable experience working with the communities they will eventually serve, learning firsthand about the complexity of the social issues that need to be addressed. Community outreach activities, involving residents in the process, help to expose students to the real living conditions and provide hands-on, informal learning, collaboration, and interaction with all actors involved. A number of housing studios have already undertaken such initiatives, fostering a form of participatory design approach that engages students with communities and the respective users, agents, and stakeholders. The participation of citizens and communities in the processes to shape the living environment has gradually become a goal shared by schools around the world. In this context, universities can play an important role in bringing together multiple actors, fields, and interests to create more inclusive and socially sustainable living environments.

On one hand, an efficient interaction with the community contributes to forge links between the university and the local communities; by embedding learning activities in the social and physical milieu, it becomes possible to bridge the gap between the culture of the place and academic training. On the other hand, it can foster an understanding of the local communities' needs by making their experiences, interests, and their own efforts to improve their housing more salient to future architects. Such outreach activities have the potential to broaden the knowledge base of the housing studio beyond the academic boundaries and reveal the specific shape of local contexts.[11]

The live project learning, however, is not only about developing skills and attitudes relevant to the needs of professions and communities. By working outside of the confines of established practices and by critically reflecting on their actions, the students inhabit potentially powerful liminal locations between theory and practice, university and community, designing and making, potentially creating new knowledge in the process. Live project pedagogy acknowledges an evolving, socially constructed curriculum that exposes competing power relations without being in opposition to more typical academic projects; live project work rather acts as a powerful complement to traditional academic programs. Live project learning inhabits a threshold space between the 'normal' activities of higher education, professional education, and professional practice, and thus provides the opportunity to critique and also re-energize the official worlds of each, in which knowledge is not just passed on but is actively created.

Housing Design as a Process of Thinking
To accomplish all these normative goals, it is necessary to train housing designers differently. There is a need to rethink and expand

11 It should be noted that such an approach entails community outreach and participation, intensive fieldwork, and development of design proposals—activities that are indeed time-consuming. Furthermore, a risk of community-based studios is that that they may raise unrealistic expectations in individuals or communities as they often represent academic, albeit creative exercises, and remain unrealized. Therefore, it is ethical and important that the studio instructors and students explain the nature and expected outcome of the studio to community groups or other stakeholders.

12 Experiential learning refers to learning in which the learner is directly in touch with the realities being studied. This goes along the line of thought of several eminent education theorists and can be traced back to the famous dictum of Confucius around 450 BC "Tell me and I will forget. Show me and I may remember. Involve me and I will understand."

13 Wink (2005) describes three models of pedagogy, the transmission model, the generative model, and the transformative model. In the transmission model the teacher transmits information directly into students. The teacher is the provider of knowledge, and the student's job is to receive and memorize that knowledge. In the generative model, the students are more involved in learning, and the process is more interactive. Students are expected to generate questions in order to direct their learning, but the teacher is still the provider of knowledge, explaining about learning. In the transformative model, the students and the teacher are partners in the learning process, actively involved in real world settings. Wink proposes that this is the most effective type of learning, that in this setting students are actively involved and interested, and are able to take knowledge they learn and transform it into new ideas, thus the model describes this kind of learning as creating knowledge.

the scope and content of housing design pedagogy, particularly studios and other design-based exercises. Future housing designers have to acquire ways that allow them to visualize and understand different settings in the city: experience, hear, and learn from different and diverse publics; and to devise spatial solutions that respond to various needs.

Acknowledging that there is a tremendous diversity of contents, approaches, and methods in housing studio pedagogy, this section advocates that an experiential learning approach needs to also be fostered.[12] A transformative model of architectural pedagogy is needed where the students and the teacher are partners in the learning process, actively involved in real-world settings.[13] Studio practices that promote the learning of process as a main objective may succeed in preparing students to effectively address rapidly changing and complex living environments in a context of collaboration and interaction with other subject matters, disciplines, and actors. In an integrative and open design studio environment, architecture students can develop skills and abilities to combine knowledge derived from different fields, disciplines, and scales, that will gradually inform their design proposals. They can also establish multiple lines of inquiry through a rich approach that draws on a variety of sources. Housing studio education can address questions posed by society not as fixed and well-defined problems, but as ways to investigate how social and life patterns evolve, to then intervene with their designs.

All the challenges that the housing studio faces today may not necessarily be a threat to the architecture profession but rather a positive evolution, an opportunity for reflection and renewal. The overwhelming changes that impact the professional and the educational environments create a common ground for experimentation. There is an obvious need for creative alternatives to current architectural education, for learning environments that can bridge across disciplinary and institutional boundaries and can facilitate an open, flexible, and integrative design process which takes into consideration the diversity of factors and different types of knowledge, values, and stakeholders involved in the creation of contemporary living environments (Charalambous, 2012).

Studio educators need to identify ways through which current housing studio practices can embrace a culture of interActions to proactively address, adapt, and respond to change. This way, the future generation of architects can acquire the design-thinking skills needed to deal effectively with a complex, multi-layered and unstable living environment and profession. The housing studio needs to provide interFaces and interActions between the individual student and the team; between different disciplines; between academia, the profession, and the community; and between global driving forces and local contexts. Emerging concerns about current educational approaches in the housing studio in particular, and the studio culture in general, present new and exciting opportunities for educators and institutions to respond to the ongoing changes in the living environments and to contribute to the transformation of the architectural profession.

References

Anthony, K. H. (1991) *Design Juries on Trial: The Renaissance of the Design Studios.* New York, NY: Van Nostrand Reinhold.

Billari, F. C., Kohler, H. P., Andersson, G., & Lundström, H. (2007) "Approaching the Limit: Long-Term Trends in Late and Very Late Fertility," in *Population and Development Review, 33*(1), 149–170.

Boyer, E. L. & Mitgang, L. D. (1996) *Building Community: A New Future for Architecture Education and Practice. A Special Report.* Ewing, NJ: California Princeton Fulfillment Services.

Bongaarts, J. (2006) "How Long Will We Live?" in *Population and Development Review, 32*(4), 605–628.

Charalambous, N., & Phocas, M. C. (2012). *Research Based Design: Interdisciplinarity and Integration of Multiple Types of Knowledge.* In Els De Vos, Johan De Walsche & Marjan Michels (eds.), *Design: Architectural Research Made Explicit in the Design Studio.* Belgium: ASP–Academic & Scientific Publishers, 275–282.

Charalambous, N. (2017). "The Challenge of Change in Living Environments: Implications and Opportunities for Architectural Education," in L. Madrazo (ed.), "Global Dwelling: Intertwining Research, Pedagogy and Community Participation." Barcelona: Editorial Enginyeria i Arquitectura La Salle, 166–178.

Cassio, M.B. (2011) "Architectural Design Studio and the Real World Out There: An Investigation of Content in Architectural Design Studio at Three Faculties of Architecture in Australia from Years 1–5," PhD thesis, The University of Melbourne.

Habraken, J. (2007) "To Tend a Garden: Thoughts on the Strenghts and Limits of Design Pedagogy," in A. Salama, & N. Wilkinson (eds.), *Design Studio Pedagogy: Horizons for the Future.* Gateshead, UK: Urban International Press Editor, 11–20.

Charalambous, N. (2014) "Research in the Design Studio: Housing Studies," in K. Hadjri (ed.), *Readings on Contemporary Housing Research,* Oikonet, 43–51. Retrieved from oikonet.wordpress.com/2014/12/17/reader1/.

Hickey, S. and Mohan, G. (2004) *Participation: From Tyranny to Transformation? Exploring New Approaches to Participation in Development.* London: Zed Books.

Charalambous, N. & Phocas, M. C. (2012) "Research in the Studio: Integrated, Research Based Design Process," in E. De Vos, J. De Walsche, M. Michels, & S. Verbruggen (eds.), *Theory by Design: Architectural Research Made Explicit in the Design Studio.* Belgium: ASP—Academic & Scientific Publishers, 289–296.

Colomina, B., Choi, E., González, I. G., & Meister, A. M. (2012) "Radical Pedagogies in Architectural Education," in *The Architectural Review.* Retrieved from architectural-review.com/today/radical-pedagogies-in-architectural-education/8636066.article

Cook, B. & Kothari, U. (2001) *Participation: The New Tyranny,* London: Zed Books.

Cunningham, A. (2005) "Notes on Education and Research around Architecture," in *The Journal of Architecture, 10*(4), 415–441.

Dorst, K. (2008). "Design Research: A Revolution-Waiting-to-Happen," in *Design Studies, 29*(1), 4–11.

Dutton, T. A. (1991) "The Hidden Curriculum and the Design Studio," in T. A. Dutton (ed.), *Voices in Architectural Education: Cultural Politics and Pedagogy.* New York, NY: Bergin & Garvey, 165–194.

Fokkema, T. & Liefbroer, A. C. (2008) "Trends in Living Arrangements in Europe: Convergence or Divergence?" in *Demographic Research, 19,* 1351–1418. Retrieved from demographic-research.org/volumes/vol19/36/19-36.pdf.

Hanson, J. (1998) *Decoding Homes and Houses.* Cambridge: Cambridge University Press.

Jeffrey, H. & Kinoshita, I. (2007) "Bridging Community Differences through Informal Processes: Re-examining Participatory Planning in Seattle and Matsudo" in *Journal of Planning Education and Research*, 26(3), 301–314.

Koch, A., Shwennsen, K., Dutton, T. A., & Smith, D. (2002). *The Redesign of Studio Culture: A Report of the AIAS Studio Culture Task Force.* Washington, DC: American Institute of Architecture Students.

Lefaivre, L. & Tzonis, A. (2012) *Architecture of Regionalism in the Age of Globalization: Peaks and Valleys in the Flat World.* Oxford: Routledge.

Lefas, P. (2009) *Dwelling and Architecture: From Heidegger to Koolhaas.* Berlin: Jovis Verlag.

Maloutas, T. & Fujita, K. (eds.) (2012) *Residential Segregation in Comparative Perspective: Making Sense of Contextual Diversity.* New York, NY: Ashgate Publishing, Ltd.

Marcuse, P. & Van Kempen, R. (eds.) (2000) *Globalizing Cities: A New Spatial Order?* London & Cambridge: Blackwell Publishers. Retrieved from homepages. gac.edu/~mbjellan/documents/MarcuseReview_001.pdf

Salama, A. (2008) "A Theory for Integrating Knowledge in Architectural Design Education," in *ArchNet-IJAR: International Journal of Architectural Research* 2, no. 1.

Sanoff, H. (2007) "Community Based Design Learning: Democracy and Collective Decision Making," in A. Salama & N. Wilkinson (eds.) *Design Studio Pedagogy: Horizons for the Future.* Gateshead, UK: Urban International Press.

Schön, D. (1985) *The Design Studio: Architecture and the Higher Learning, an Exploration of its Traditions and Potentials.* London: RIBA Publications for RIBA Building Industry Trust.

Schön, D. (1988) "Toward a Marriage of Artistry & Applied Science in the Architectural Design Studio," in *Journal of Architectural Education,* 41, 4–10.

Tzonis, A. (2014). "A Framework for Architectural Education," in *Frontiers of Architectural Research*, 3(4), 477–479.

UNESCO/UIA (2005) "UNESCO/UIA Charter for Architectural Education," Retrieved from http://uia-architectes.org/image/PDF/CHARTES/CHART_ANG.pdf.

Van Schaik. L (2008), *Spatial Intelligence: New Futures for Architecture*, Chicester, UK: Wiley.

Wink, J. (2005). *Critical Pedagogy: Notes from the Real World.* Boston, MA: Prentice Hall.

INTER

The house is rightly considered one of the most important means of exploring the social and experiential dimensions of architecture. Houses are a complex expression of the everyday life of their inhabitants, of different cultures, ethnicities, and social groups and are often described as "sociograms," not only of their occupants but also of society at large. Understanding the ways in which the home, as a spatial form, relates to the social, the cultural, and the individual in the context of the increasingly divided, complex, and differentiated experiences of contemporary life, is one of the central challenges of the housing design studio.

Having as a starting point the complexity of factors that have shaped living environments in cities though time, the studio approach seeks to explore, understand, and map uncertainties that shape contemporary urban living and housing in particular in a critical manner; unveil critical concerns on the impact of such unsettling practices on the design and production of living environments; and foster and embrace a culture of interFaces between the individ-

FACES

ual student and the team; between different disciplines; between academia, the profession, and the community; and between global common driving forces and local contexts.

The housing studio at UCY aims to develop processes, knowledge, and skills that will enable future professionals to contribute to well-designed, well-planned, equitable, sustainable, and socially inclusive living environments in order to proactively adapt and respond to contemporary uncertain conditions. Many of the projects presented in this section are conceptualized as a form of transformative pedagogy, based around experiential learning, which is located between two worlds, the university and the community. Central to the studio's methodology is, therefore, an action research and evidence-based approach that focuses on issues defined by a nuanced understanding of the context in its broader sense, which includes the economic, social, and spatial spheres as well as the network of the agents/stakeholders involved.

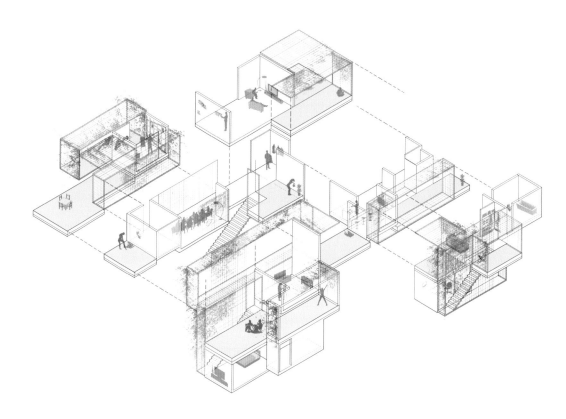

Frames of Sharing

Irini Klidara

This project is located in a mixed-use area that used to be a famous tourist destination in the city of Famagusta. The proposal addresses the concept of cohabitation between a family relocating in the post-conflict city and the tourists, who have always been a large majority of the city's transient population as well as a major source of income. Building on the Cypriot's strong sense of hospitality and speculating the city's future users, a family dwelling is proposed that can also provide an alternative, small-scale, temporary accommodation for the tourists. A major challenge addressed by this dwelling is the coexistence of the family's everyday life with the arrival of the temporary inhabitants during the summer months. The project confronts this issue through a sequence of overlapping frames/spaces and their spatial configuration, which enables multiple circulation options that are controlled through movable partitions. This facilitates the creation of a private sleeping area for the tourists as well as the maintenance of the family's spatial needs and privacy. Additionally, it provides spaces for sharing activities between the permanent and temporary users of the house. Issues of adaptation, flexibility, privacy, and shared living are explored.

Famagusta profile

Water Sports | Leisure | Housing | Economic Activities & Sports | Sightseeing

Sequence of overlapping voids

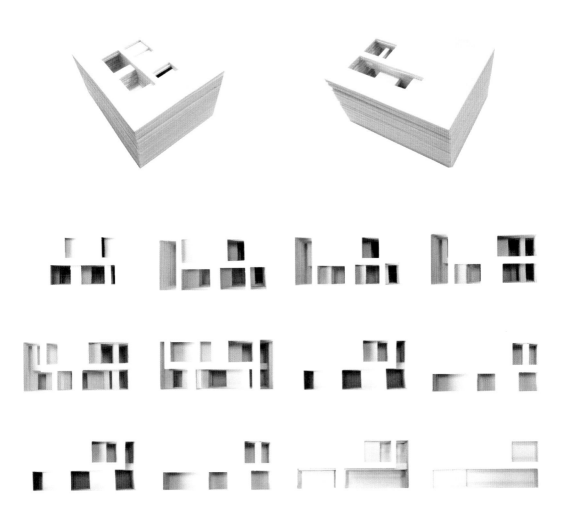

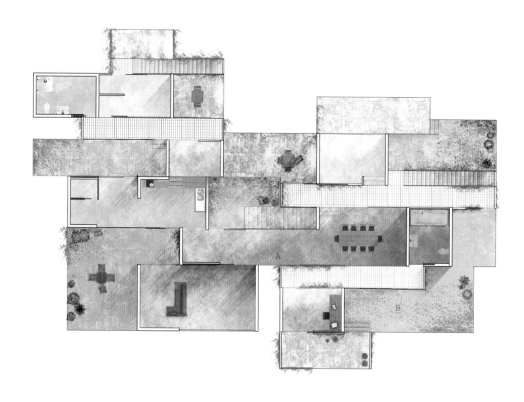

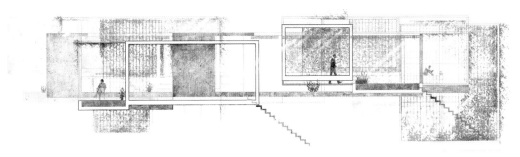

Section A

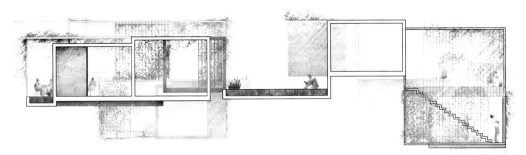

Section B

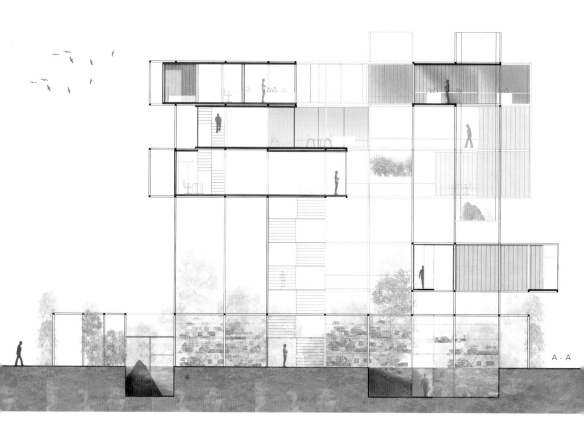

A - A

ResurrACT

Stefanos Kyprianou

The project explores the relationship between housing and issues emerging from the rehabilitation of the "ghost" city of Famagusta. The structural decay, the contaminated soil, and the taking-over of the city by nature formulate the three themes that the project aims to address in order to render the city a liveable place. As such, the dwelling is designed to host scientists from three different disciplines that will work and live at the same time in a "machine" that will sample, document, monitor, and propose ideas for the confrontation of these issues. The design was influenced by the cooperation and conflicts arising out of the scientists' working activities and their daily domestic needs. The project addresses the need for varying degrees of privacy defining the public, semi-private, and private realms which are organized in different but overlapping levels. The ground floor is designed as the public space and is organized both as an archive and as an open exhibition for the public to observe and engage in the scientists' work. The structure is comprised of steel tubes joined vertically and horizontally, as a temporary scaffolding, allowing it to be partially or completely disassembled when the scientists' needs change or their work is completed.

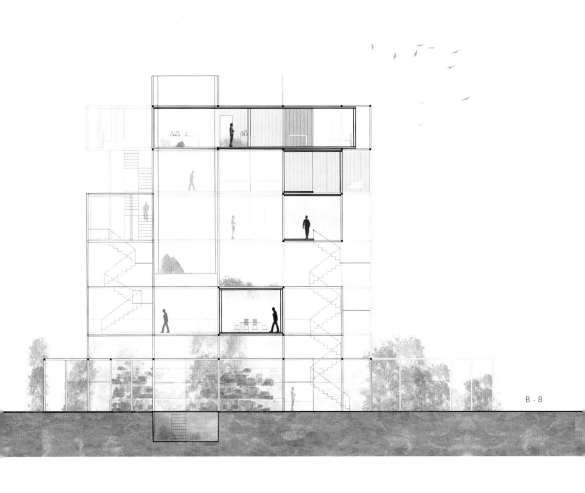

B - B

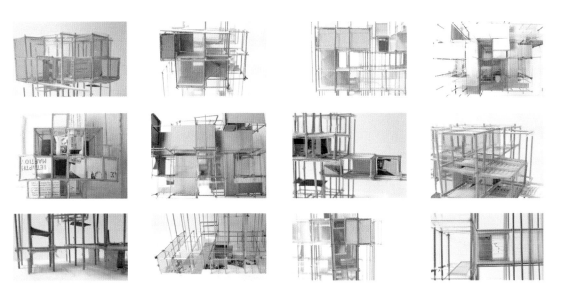

1st Floor

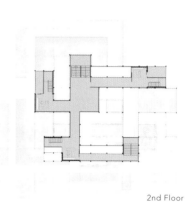

2nd Floor

3rd Floor

4th Floor

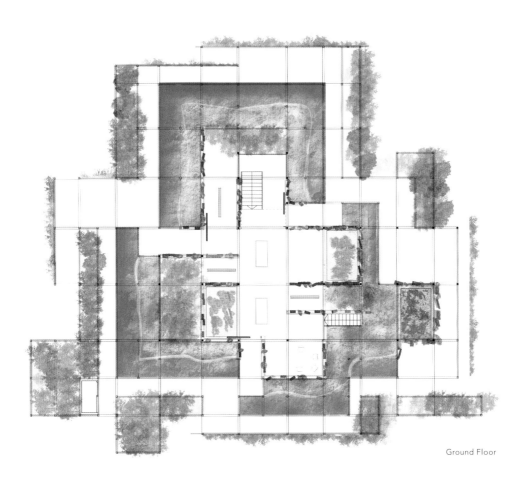

Ground Floor

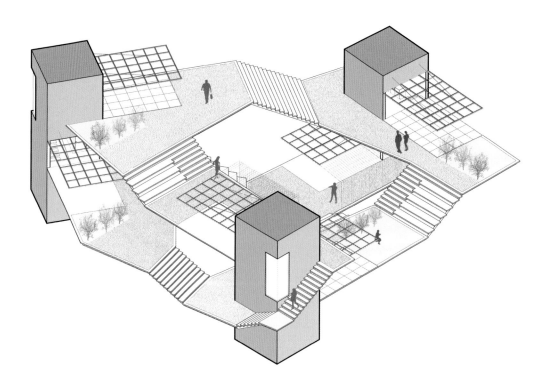

Living in Motion

Andreas Konstaninou

The rehabilitation of a post-conflict environment such as Famagusta poses a number of challenges. The possible scenarios are numerous as well as uncertain; diverse users with different needs (socially, ethnically) and different living patterns may return to live in the city. The traditional concept of housing in such a context is therefore challenged and needs to be reconsidered. This projects sets out to explore the potential of a universal and standardized unit that will be able to continuously adjust and adapt in order to accommodate a variety of different potential inhabitants. The scenarios were developed according to different age groups and working statuses.

The concept of "flexibility" in everyday living as well as in architecture is explored. The project consists of fixed cores and a continuous surface that serves as the circulation, public space, and expansion area of the units. The fixed core accommodates the spatially fixed activities of the house such as the sanitary services and the kitchen, whereas a horizontal metal grid serves as a flexible/adaptable space that the inhabitants can appropriate according to their individual needs. The areas in between the units are conceived as an extension/continuation of the street pattern, encouraging social interaction between the complex's inhabitants and the local citizens.

Unit for a student

Spatial Arrangment × Activities

Circulation × Public/Private

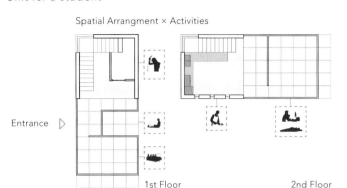
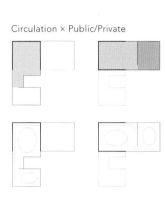

Entrance ▷   1st Floor   2nd Floor

Unit for two students

Spatial Arrangment × Activities

Circulation × Public/Private

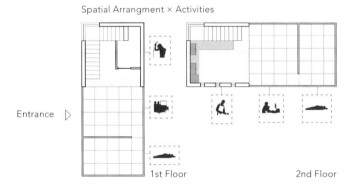
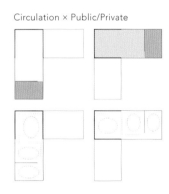

Entrance ▷   1st Floor   2nd Floor

Work at home

Spatial Arrangment × Activities

Circulation × Public/Private

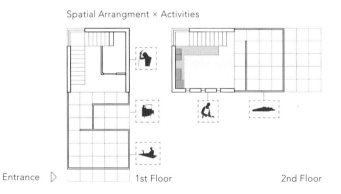
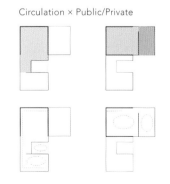

Entrance ▷   1st Floor   2nd Floor

Legend   Shower Relax Work Sleep Study Cook   Shared   Private

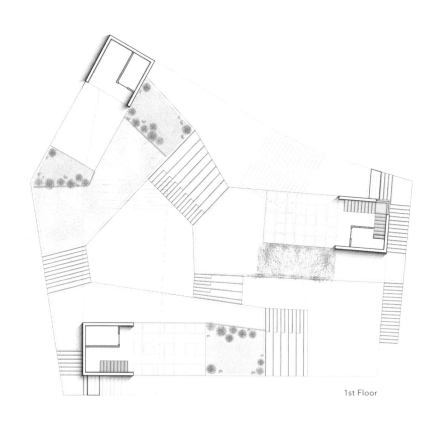

1st Floor

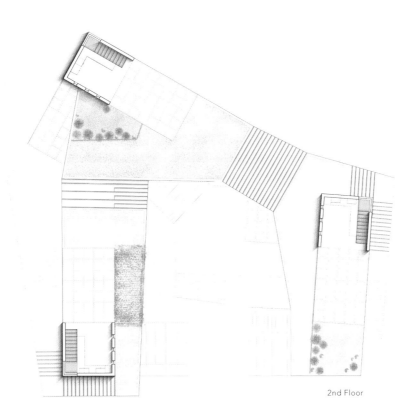

2nd Floor

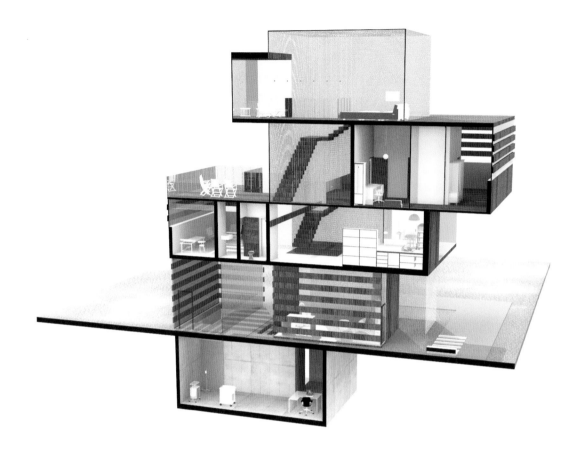

Shifting Boundaries

Lefteris Kaimakliotis

The project aims to address the uncertain conditions with which the inhabitants of a post-conflict environment may be confronted in their everyday lives. These include the need to address diverse users and uses at different scales in the city—in a neighborhood as well as in a housing unit—and the need to live and work in the same place in an attempt to bring the city back to life. The project aims to confront these often-conflicting factors by proposing a house that fosters diversity in new and productive ways in the city of Famagusta. The inhabitants of the house, a family with kids, work at home, practicing quite different occupations. At the same time, their home has the capacity to accommodate guests during the summer season, since Famagusta is speculated to regain its former touristic character. The public activities are located on the ground and first floor of the house and the private ones on the above floors. Vertical circulation serves as the mechanism of regulating the conflicting needs of the house's inhabitants, such as public/private activities, home/work space.

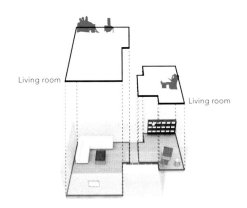

Living room

Living room

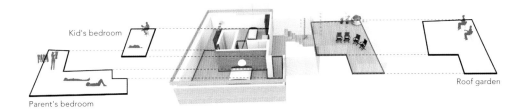

Kid's bedroom

Parent's bedroom

Roof garden

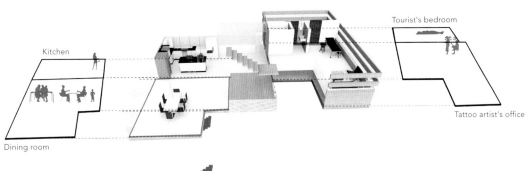

Kitchen

Tourist's bedroom

Dining room

Tattoo artist's office

Lawyer's office

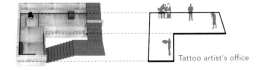

Tattoo artist's office

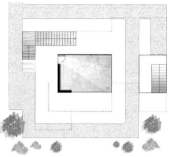

1st Floor

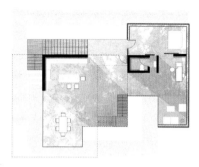

2nd Floor

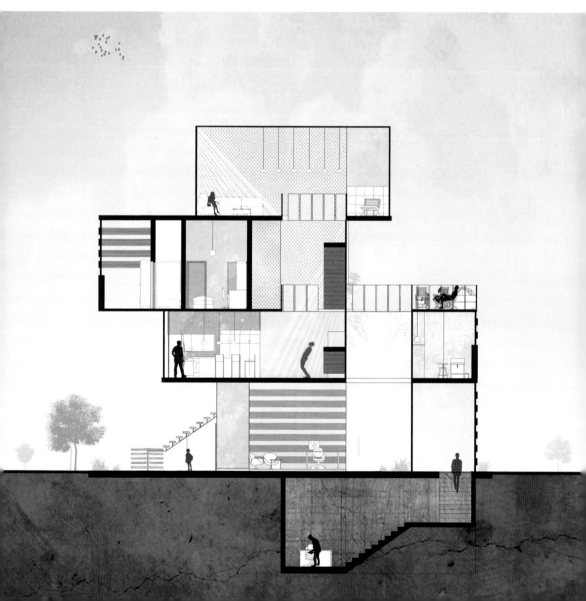

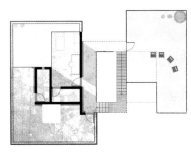

3rd Floor

4th Floor

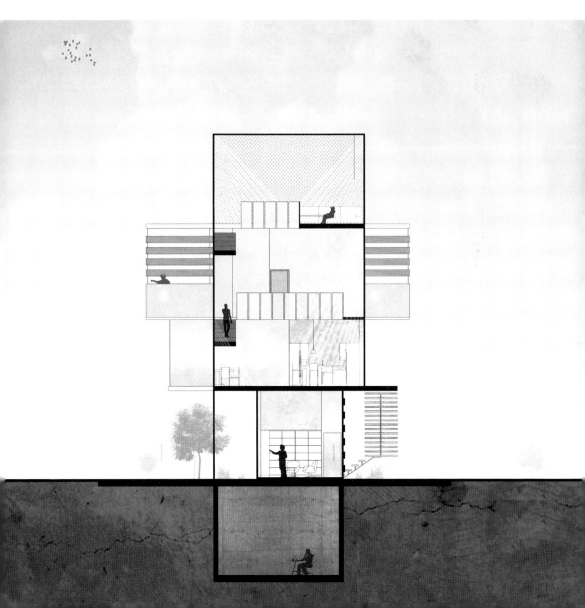

THE SITE

LIMASSOL WESTERN AREA NEAR LIMASSOL MARINA.

INTERVIEWING SOME THE INHABITANTS OF THIS SETTLEMENT SHOWED THAT THE EXISTING HOUSES ARE DAMAGED BEYOND REPAIR, SO THEIR REPLACEMENT COULD HELP IMPROVE THE EVERYDAY LIFE OF THE INHABITANTS, ESPECIALLY THOSE WHO SPEND MOST OF THEIR TIME AT HOME.

AREA MAIN FEATURES:
· PREVIOUSLY INDUSTRIAL AREA (GRADUALLY BEING ABANDONED)
· INCREASING TOURISTIC ACTIVITY
· RESIDENTIAL AREA.
· MOSTLY LOCAL REFUGEE SETTLEMENTS
· A LARGE PART OF THE AREA PREOWNED | BY TURKISH-CYPRIOTS. INHARITED
· ADJACENT TO THE OLD CITY OF LIMASSOL.

AREA HOUSING MAIN FEATURES:
- REFUGEE SETTLEMENTS - STANDARDISED HOUSES
- PRIVATE APARTMENT BLOCKS
- MUNICIPAL APARTMENT BLOCKS
- DETACHED HOUSES.

CHOICE OF SPECIFIC FIELD:
VARIOUS NEW HOUSING PROGRAMS CAN BE SUPPORTED IN THAT AREA BUT THIS REQUIRES THE CONSERVATION OF THE EXISTING ONES.

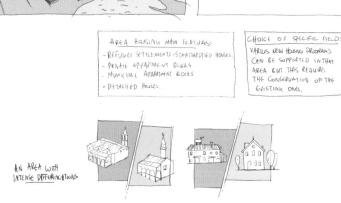

AN AREA WITH INTENSE DIFFERENTIATIONS

UN[Stable] House

Anastasia Psoma, Michalis Psaras,
Aristofanis H'charalambous

The project argues that a dwelling is no longer a permanent and static structure as it has traditionally been in small communities such as Cyprus. The inhabitants and their needs are constantly changing and thus a house should be able to adjust and adapt through time.

Through an empirical, evidence-based study that included interviews with existing inhabitants, mapping the existing living conditions, and photographing surveys that took place at the neighborhood under study, a series of complex issues emerged. In the area of the western neighborhoods in the city of Limassol, families live under poor conditions in subsidized houses that longer correspond to their needs. Due to lack of space they are either forced to live in congested conditions or in some cases to temporarily extend their backyards or informally use the streetfronts in order to respond to basic needs.

The existing inhabitants could benefit from a new affordable, expandable, and adaptable house that could address their individual as well as their collective needs. As such, the public space forms an important aspect of the proposed design, providing space for activities and interaction already embedded in their everyday patterns of living. Additionally, the low-income inhabitants could take advantage of the possibility to rent a space in their house to tourists or temporary residents for a short period of time. Each unit of the proposed housing com-

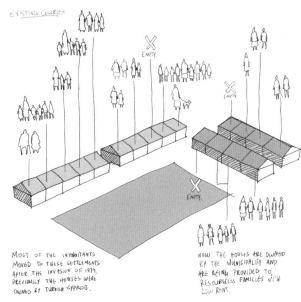

MOST OF THE INHABITANTS MOVED TO THESE SETTLEMENTS AFTER THE INVASION OF 1974. PREVIOUSLY THE HOUSES WERE OWNED BY TURKISH-CYPRIOTS.

NOW THE HOUSES ARE OWNED BY THE MUNICIPALITY AND ARE BEING PROVIDED TO RESOURCELESS FAMILIES WITH LOW RENT.

plex is designed in such a way as to maintain its privacy on one hand but at the same time be integrated with the common areas, where all planned and unplanned social activities can take place (barbeque nights, patios for socializing, green areas).

The proposed main permanent structure is steel frame (I-beams) placed on a 1.5-meter grid creating a universal structural system. Each frame is designed in order to have the capacity to be filled with panels of different materials (polycarbonate, plywood, glass, metal, and concrete blocks), depending on the needs of its owner. It also allows the inhabitants to easily add or remove panels, creating or dismantling spaces. Three distinct proposals were created according to the design principles and needs of the users that emerged from the field study and site analysis. The housing units are organized parallel to each other with in-between public spaces for both the inhabitants and the neighborhood. The open space is organized in green areas and activity areas, where customized grid structures are placed, facilitating and encouraging a variety of activities to take place.

ALTHOUGH THE PURPOSE OF THIS COMPLEX IS TO ACCOMMODATE RESOURCELESS PEOPLE, NO NEW FAMILIES COME TO RENT A HOME BECAUSE OF THE BAD CONDITION OF THE STRUCTURES.

THE BAD FINANCIAL CONDITION OF THE FAMILIES AND THE POORLY MAINTAINED SETTLEMENTS MAKES THE COMPLEX UNINHABITABLE FOR LIVING.

THE SPIRIT OF A COMMUNAL HOUSING COMPLEX IS SLOWLY FADING AWAY. HOWEVER MANY YOUNG COUPLES OR FAMILIES SEEK A CHEAPER SOLUTION FOR THEIR HOUSE.

THE COMPLEX IS GRADUALLY BEING ABANDONED

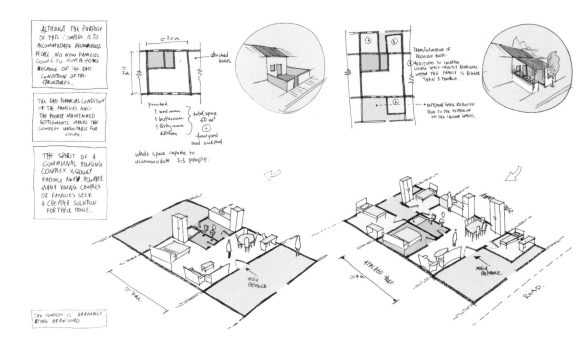

provided.
1 bedroom
1 bathroom
1 living room
kitchen
} total space 50 m² (+) frontyard and backyard

Whole space capable to accommodate 2-3 people.

attached house

TRANSFORMATION OF PROVIDED HOUSE.
ADDITIONS TO INCREASE LIVING SPACE -MOSTLY BEDROOMS WHEN THE FAMILY IS BIGGER THAN 3 PEOPLE.

• OUTDOOR SPACE REDUCED DUE TO THE EXPANSION OF THE INDOOR SPACES.

MAIN ENTRANCE

ATTACHED HOUSE

MAIN ENTRANCE

ROAD

DESIGN PRINCIPLES

- A KIT OF VARIOUS POSSIBLE FILLINGS WINDOWS, SOLID WALLS, WOOD, MESH FABRIC etc THAT CAN GIVE MANY DIFFERENT RELIEF TO THE PROVIDED SPACE

- THE STEEL FRAME

- DEVELOPMENT INTO STEPS

- REINFORCE THE COMMUNAL SPIRIT. COMMON ACTIVITIES BETWEEN HOUSES.

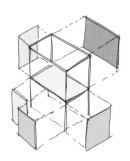

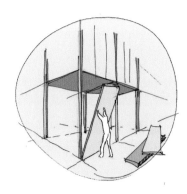

PROJECT OBJECTIVES:

• AFFORDABILITY. - PEOPLE WITH LOW INCOME
• EXPANDABILITY - CONVERTABILITY
• CREATE A SMALL COMMUNITY- SUPPORT BETWEEN INHABITANTS.
• CREATE STRONGER BONDS WITH THE COMPLEX AND WITH THE CITY.

GIVING THE USER THE OPPORTUNITY TO MANIPULATE THE FILLINGS OF THE FRAME, CHOOSING FROM A VARIETY OF TRANSPARENT OR NON TRANSPARENT, SOFT OR HARD MATERIALS THE STRUCTURE CAN BE TRANSFORMED INTO MANY POSSIBLE APPROACHES

AS THE HOUSES ARE NOT DESIGNED FOR A SPECIFIC USER THEY HAVE TO BE ADAPTABLE TO EACH INHABITANT'S NEEDS.

TO ACHIEVE THIS THE PROJECT IS BASED ON A BASIC STRUCTURE PROVIDING THE STANDARD SPACES (LIVING DINING, COOKING, BATHROOM BEDROOM, OUTDOOR PRIVATE SPACE.)

THINKING ABOUT THE PROPOSAL

HOUSE EXPANSIONS:
- INCREASING INDOOR SPACE
- BUILT WITH CHEAP AFFORTABLE MATERIALS
- OUTDOOR SPACE
- MOSTLY ACCOMMODATE TEMPORARY ACTIVITIES AND SOMETIMES REMAIN VACANT-UNUSED
- DECREASE OF OUTDOOR SPACE

EXTRA SPACE ADDED TO THE COMPLEX CAN BE USED FOR A COMMON ACTIVITY THAT CAN PROVIDE EXTRA INCOME TO THE INHABITANTS.

NEED OF A COMMON ACTIVITY THAT CAN REINFORCE THE PROGRAM OF THE COMPLEX AND CREATE A BETTER CONNECTION WITH THE CITY, ALSO TO PROVIDE EXTRA INCOME THAT CAN BE USED FOR COMMON GOOD.

MAIN HOUSING TYPOLOGIES ELEMENTS THAT WILL BE INCLUDED IN THE PROPOSAL.

TYPES OF USERS

ELDERS   YOUNG COUPLES

SINGLES   TOURISTS

FAMILIES

DETACHED HOUSES

PRIVATE AND GARDEN OR SPACE.

SENCE OF OWNERSHIP.

MORE ADAPTABLE TO ONE'S NEEDS

PARTICIPATION IN DESIGN

ATTACHED HOUSES

ACCOMMODATING A LARGER NUMBER OF PEOPLE IN LESS SPACE.

CLOSER RELATIONSHIP BETWEEN NEIGHBORS.

CREATION OF A COMMUNAL SPIRIT - A LARGE FAMILY.

Single person

studio

Single bedroom

two person - couple   duplex

COMMON CIRCULATION SYSTEM.

family   family apartment.

NUMBER OF BEDROOMS - PRIVATE SPACE VARIES ACCORDING TO THE NUMBER OF INHABITANTS.

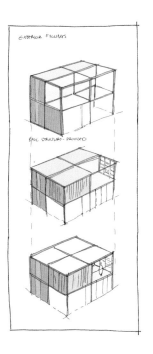

EXTERIOR FILLINGS

BASIC STRUCTURE - PROVIDED

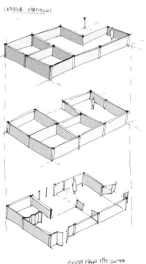

INTERIOR PARTITIONS

EXCEPT FROM THE OUTER SHELL OF THE HOUSE THE INSIDE ARRANGEMENT OF EACH UNIT CAN BE CHANGED BY ADDING OR REMOVING THE INTERIOR PARTITION SURFACES.

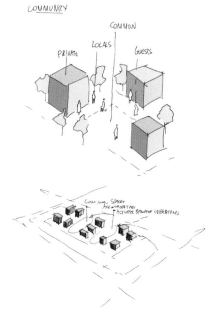

COMMUNITY

COMMON

PRIVATE   LOCALS   GUESTS

COMMON SPACE ACCOMMODATING ACTIVITIES BETWEEN INHABITANTS

UN[Stable] House × 1

Michalis Psaras

The project aims to question and reinterpret the concept and design of the dwelling in the underprivileged context of the Western neighborhoods in Limassol, where access to adequate and affordable housing is becoming more difficult to guarantee for the existing diverse inhabitants. The proposed complex consists of three housing units based on an overall steel frame. The universality of the steel structure facilitates the individual appropriation of space and surfaces by the inhabitants, as deemed necessary. The only fixed areas in the houses are the service cores (kitchen and bathrooms) while parts of the frame remain free to be filled in depending on the owner's future needs for expansion. Particular emphasis is placed on the in-between open spaces, which encourage community shared activities at different scales. The inhabitants can jointly sustain their neighborhood through a profitable mechanism of hosting guests in their houses. The highest story of each house, which is also connected throught the elevated pathway, is provided for guests who can share spaces such as the kitchen and the courtyards with the hosts.

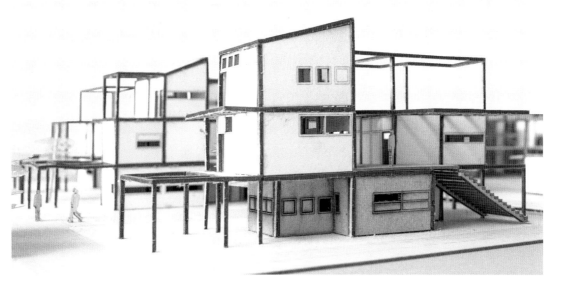

UN[Stable] House × 2

Aristofanis H'charalambous

This housing project focuses on the provision of flexible spaces that can be adjusted by each user to fulfill his/her particular needs and aspirations. The complex consists of four units, one of which is divided into two separate flats. The main feature of each house is a central shared space through which the inhabitants can access any other space in the house. This central space enhances the connection of the spaces within the house as well as the connection of the indoor spaces with the outside. Each house of the complex is arranged into six spatial enti-

ties. The central corridor is surrounded by all spaces: a double-height living space (living room, dining room), the patio, the kitchen and the bathroom (located next to each other), the bedrooms, and a guesthouse. The double-height living space allows the addition of a loft if needed. Each housing unit of the complex has a guestroom for accommodating guests and tourists, which is accessible through the paths that connect the houses both on the ground and first floor levels.

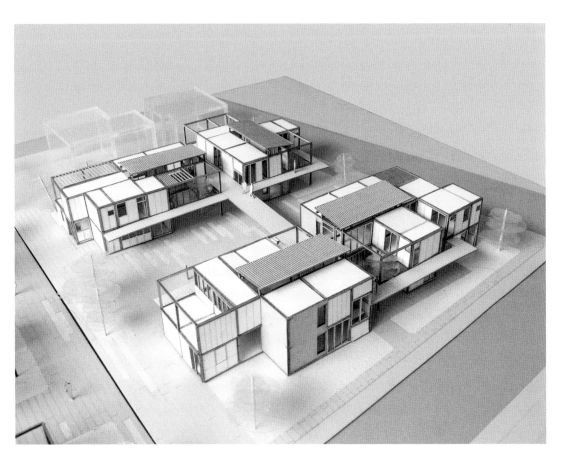

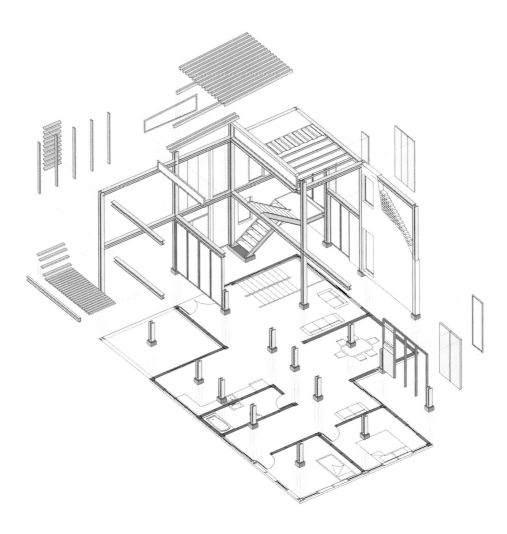

Catalogue of vertical surfaces

Thick wall
permanent

Gypsum board
non permanent

Wood panels

Transparent glass

Wood beams
(shade)

Tent fabrics

Steel mesh for
climbing plants

Bamboo
(shade, view)

Decking

Interior filling
with storage

Fabric curtain

Opaque glass

Changeable
furniture

Transformable
fillings

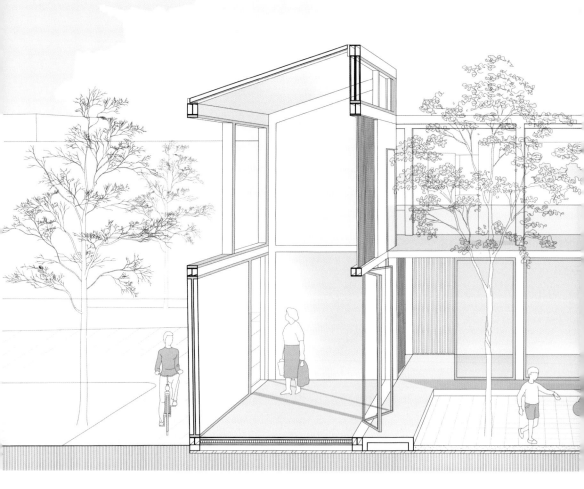

UN[Stable] House × 3

Anastasia Psoma

The inhabitants of each house no longer live permanently in the same house. Because of that, the house should be able to adapt to the needs of the current resident. The permanent structure is a steel frame with infill panels of various materials. The project aims to dissolve the monolithic cubical housing variations of the existing site and revisit the traditional Cypriot housing typology of the central courtyard with sustainable outdoor spaces. As a result, the courtyard becomes the bonding element of the house that orchestrates the external circulation from one room to another. The basic structure of the house is able to adapt to multiple room configuration scenarios through private and semi-private spaces. Another key element of the project is the idea of the guesthouse, where a private space in the upper level will be for guests, providing an additional income for the dwellers. The project is composed of four two-level housing units, tied together with an elevated walkway. The proposed form of cohabitation seeks to reinforce the bonds between the family members and suggests new relations and shared spaces among neighboring inhabitants.

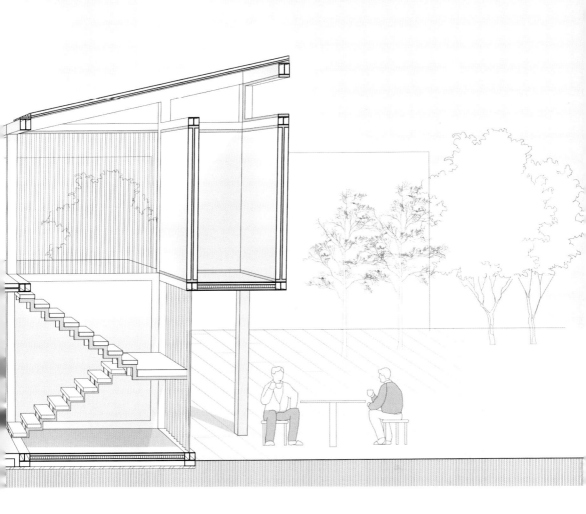

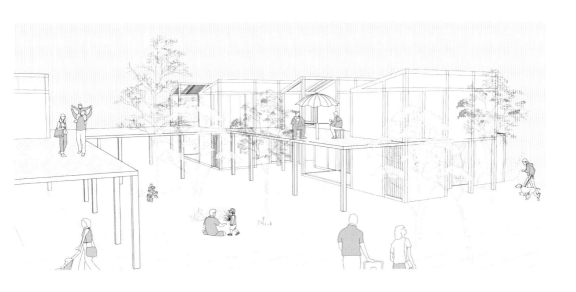

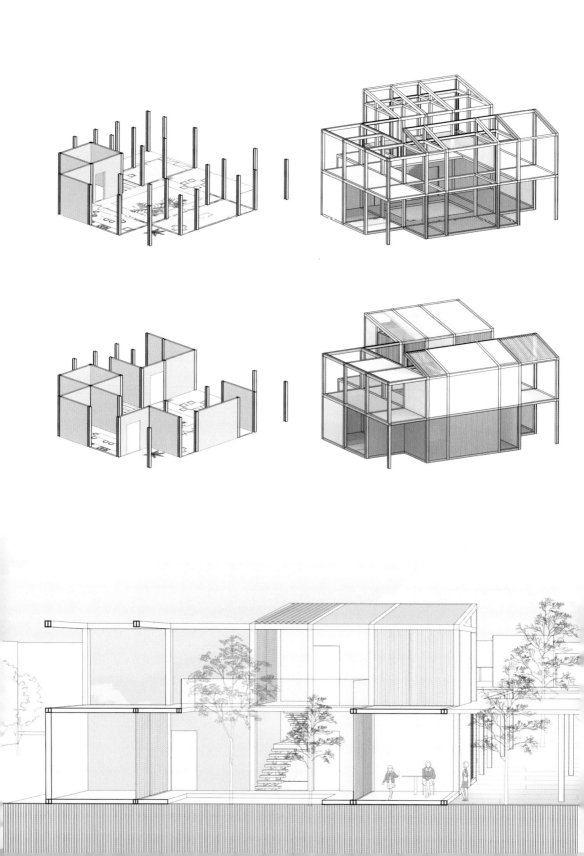

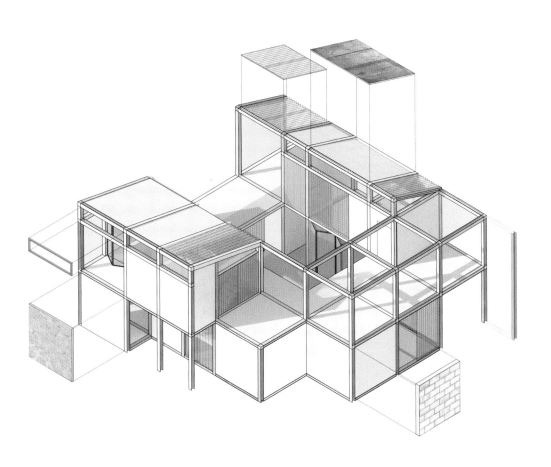

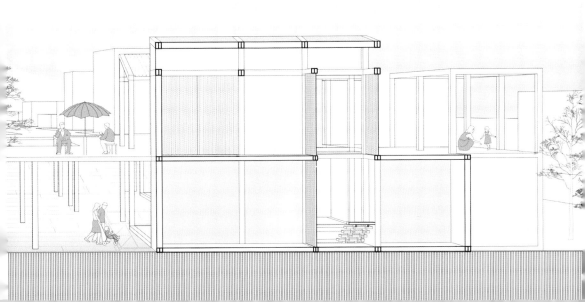

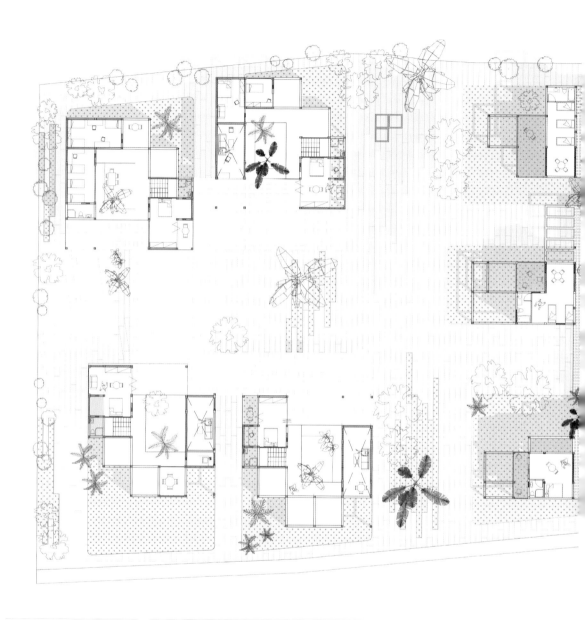

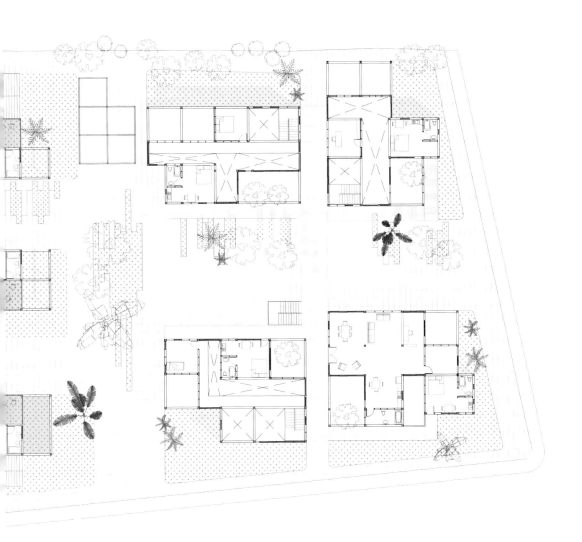

Transcendental Living

Paisios Skitini, Kateryna Chrysostomou,
Christos Dionysis

The project aims to explore forms of habitation in a non-urban environment and to redefine the relationship between humans and nature in our everyday lives. It proposes a new concept of dwelling that provides the necessary infrastructure to live and work in and with nature. The project emerged from the critical analysis of the living conditions presented in the movie *Brokeback Mountain*. Producing food through agriculture/farming is a concept which cowboys where accustomed until the 1980s. In order to revisit these notions in contemporary times, a home for two "cowboys" is proposed. The concept of layering has been the generating mechanism of the proposal. The house thus consists of parallel, overlapping strips of enclosed and open spaces, which are appropriated in different ways during each season and subsequently impact on the activities that take place indoors and outdoors. On the horizontal axis of the house three layers are most prominent: the level that touches the ground and folds underground to create the private rooms and foster a relationship with water and soil; the middle, glass layer that shapes the enclosed spaces and at the same time visually joins the inside with the outside; and the top layer of a wooden roof that protects from natural elements. Key natural elements such as light and water, in different climatic conditions through the day and throughout the seasons, form an integral part of the proposal, facilitate diverse experiences and patterns of everyday living, and promote the experience of living a "transcendental" life.

Everyday patterns in summer and winter

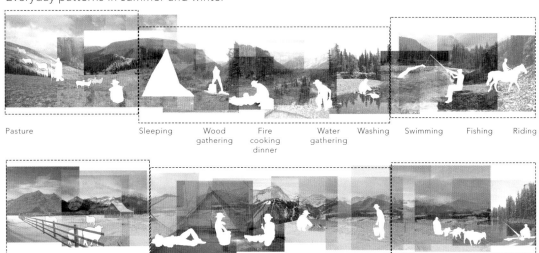

Pasture   Sleeping   Wood   Fire   Water   Washing   Swimming   Fishing   Riding
gathering   cooking   gathering
dinner

Pasture   Sleeping   Washing   Dinner   Fire   Water   Sledding   Fishing
cooking   gathering

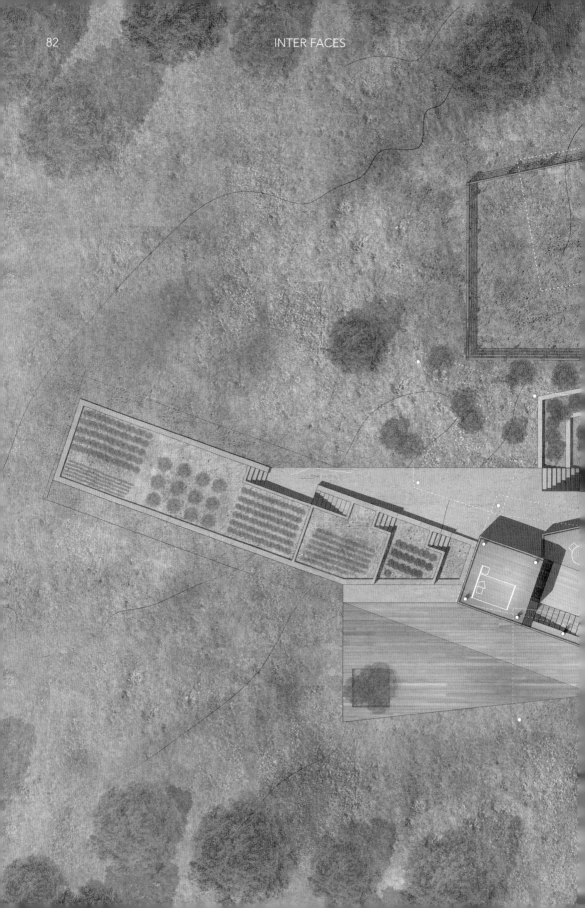

Winter Activities

Summer Activities

Collective Microworlds

Savvas Dimitriou, Mikaella Raspa, Christos Georgiou

Living conditions in certain parts of the world, such as India, are extremely complex and require an alternative approach towards thinking and designing housing. The proposal addresses the cohabitation of single mothers and their children, who constitute a large majority of the population in the study area at Darami. The project was inspired by the movie *Slumdog Millionaire*, which served as the basis to initiate an analysis of the circumstances under which such families live. The need for sharing domestic activities as a mechanism of mutual support and survival emerges. Domestic activities were thus revisited in this specific context and the concepts of private and public worlds were redefined. The project explores the spatio-temporal meanings of "sharing" and "common" through shared inhabitations within and across the scales of the housing unit, the neighborhood and the public space, responding simultaneously to the existing needs of the users and the site.

Daily routines of single mothers and their children

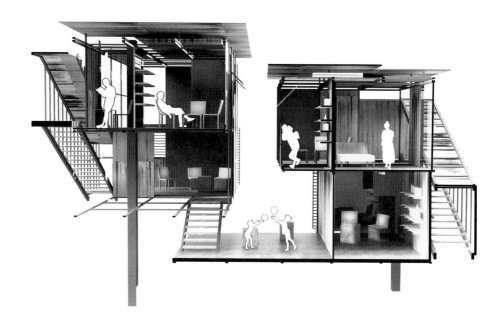

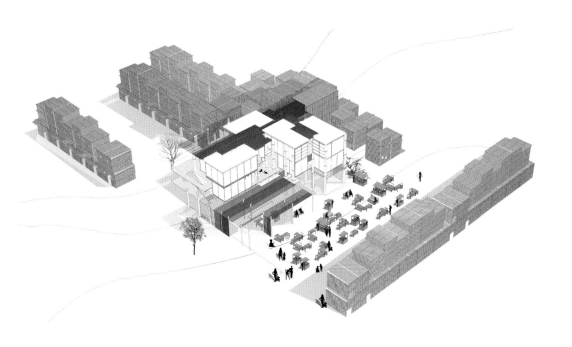

Shared Worlds

Andronikos Kalli

The project reconsiders the meanings of habitation and public space, as notions interrelated and inextricably connected with the social economic reality of each place. Contemporary life patterns seem to promote private ownership and living, resulting in the marginalization of public culture and participation while increasing insensitivity towards socio-political changes. Therefore, the project aims to explore the spatio-temporal meaning of "sharing" and "common", as a response to the circumstances of the financial crisis; and design a model of shared inhabitations within and across the scales of the housing unit, the neighborhood, and the public space, responding to the needs of the users and the site. Overall, the proposal aims to organize the space according to common activities of everyday sharing and to create the appropriate relations and connections with the existing topology and ecology so that the fragmented and alienated neighborhood can give out a sense of place and belonging. The smaller scale of the housing groups is also based on spatio-temporal transformation of public platforms, which combine both privacy and collective inhabitations of space. Spaces of primary services and activities, and spaces of undefined activities are placed between and along the shared living complexes, creating the "spatial receivers" of all common activities that can be realized and shared outside of the envelope of the private activities.

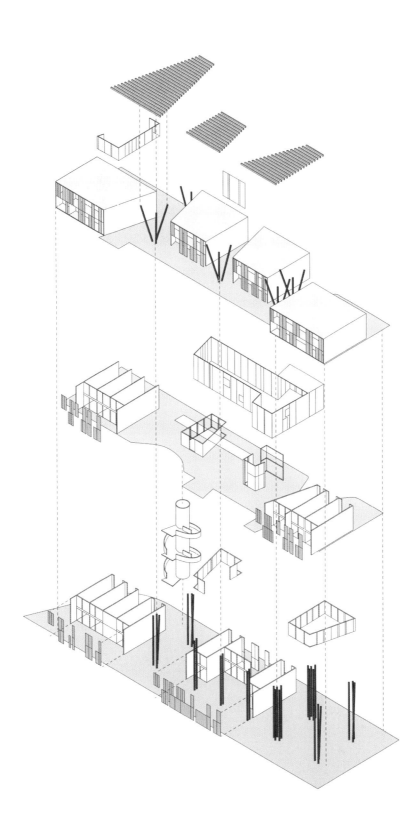

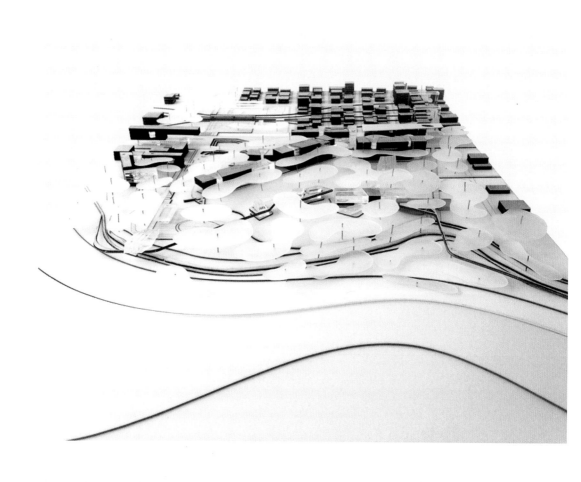

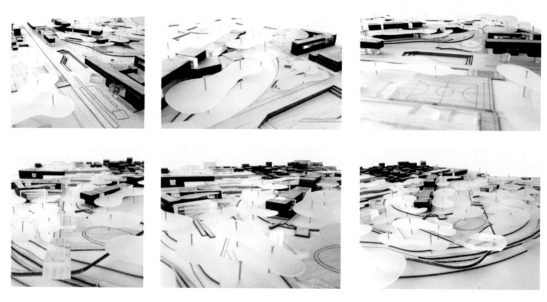

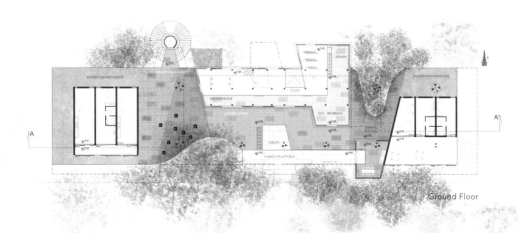

Ground Floor

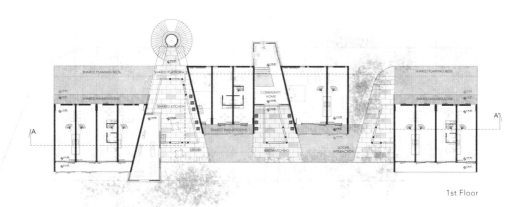

1st Floor

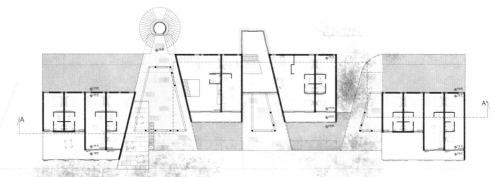

2nd Floor

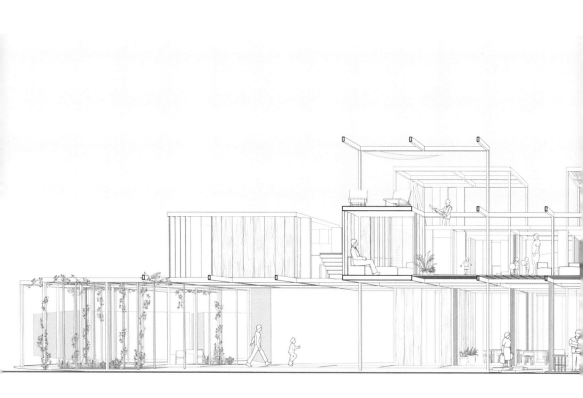

Extended Family Networks

Nasia Pantelidou

The project proposes the creation of an extended family network as a resilient housing support system. It attempts to criticize the deterioration of the concept of the neighborhood and the way of dealing with collective housing in Cyprus as a solution to the housing problem of low-income families.

The proposal attempts to offer young couples and low-income families the opportunity to acquire their first residence through a system of mutual support between the residents of the complex and the community. The project deals with the challenges of a growing family, affordability, and the appropriation and adaptation of the residence as per the profile of the individual user.

Downgraded neighborhoods with the characteristics of low financial rents and easy access to educational institutions and public transport are strategically selected in order to prevent desertification and achieve their revitalization. The community of Ayios Ioannis in Larnaca is chosen as a case study.

The proposal takes place in three phases, aiming at the smooth integration of the new inhabitants into the community, as well as their involvement and participation in the process

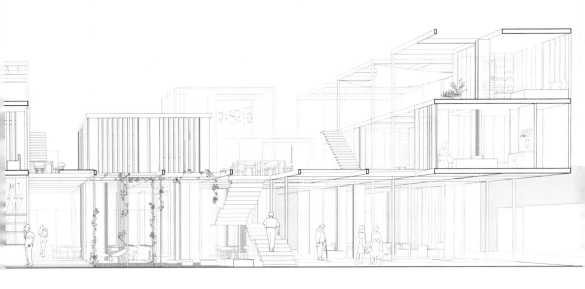

of developing the housing complex. As a first step, a workshop is set up to identify the current needs for basic services at the community level and tackle them through a series of programmatic "vaccinations."

In the second phase, the support infrastructure of the initial housing units is built through the involvement of the residents in the process of construction. The project suggests minimum dimension housing units that share activities between them, encouraging the creation of an alternative extended family network between the young couples. A grid-type building system creates the feeling of a spatial game that evolves into the third phase. Both private residential units and the common areas of the complex can be expanded and transformed to meet the residents' needs.

The ground floor hosts a workshop space, a community kitchen, and cultivation spaces. The workshop space supports the construction of the complex as well as the maintenance of the units.

Ultimately, the proposal attempts to provide a user-managed system that allows different scenarios to manage the private, communal, and public boundaries through time.

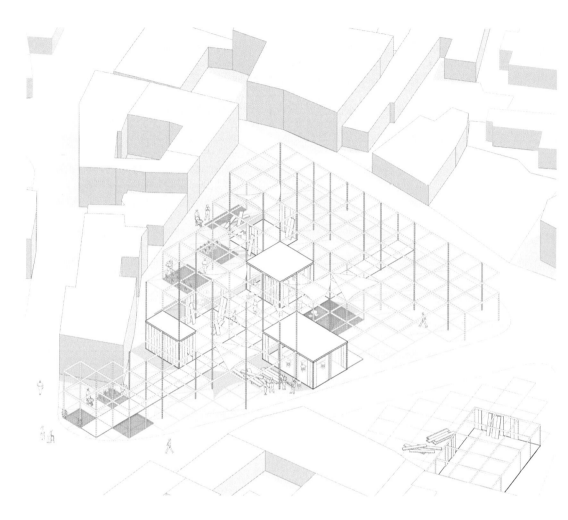

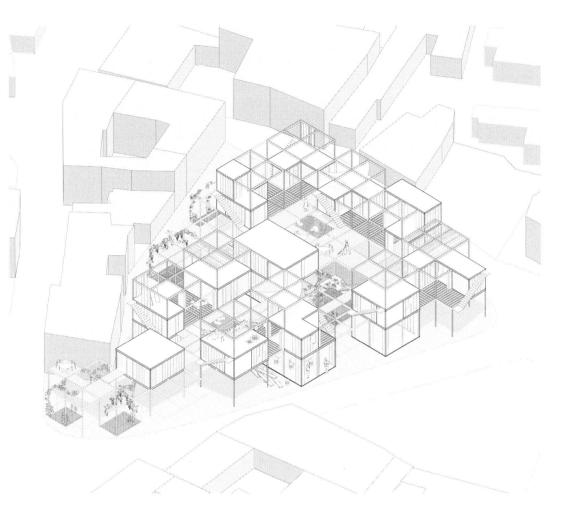

INTER

This section fosters an inquiry into potential responses to contemporary conditions of uncertainty in the form of professional practice, design, social innovation, and/or community initiatives. Housing projects developed by four architectural practices aiming at embracing a culture of interActions through complex collaborative processes while involving a number of actors representing a vast range of knowledge, experiences, and agendas are presented and discussed.

ACTIONS

The professional practices of MOS, Ateliermob, Urban Nouveau, Shigeru Ban, and the work of UN-Habitat Lebanon present a new body of work that is influenced by the new order of things/factors such as the financial and environmental crises, sociopolitical instabilities, and increased mobility. Alternative modes of practicing reveal new forms of operation in transformed contexts and for users not previously confronted.

Ateliermob

Working with the 99%

Marvila Palace Reconstruction,
Photo Francisco Nogueira

We are witnessing fast changes in contemporary life both at a global scale as well as in the local contexts. The recent financial and environmental crises, sociopolitical instabilities, and increased mobility are only a few of the issues that we architects are called to confront. How have such changes affected/influenced/shaped your work?

Architecture is always determined by its context. The question is, often, what is meant by the word "context." For us, it implies not simply the physical and/or the environmental space where it is lo-

cated but, more broadly, also social, cultural, and political perspectives. Cumulatively, it also implies where we, as individuals, situate ourselves within the practice and within the world. The beauty of it is that we are always producing contemporary culture. Even the pastiche reflects the time and context where it is brought to life. To produce architecture, one must be updated, be it on new technologies of construction or new demands that reality imposes on us. One must be conscious of the world and, for us, architecture is also, if not in the first place, an intellectual activity, and its materialization is a reflection of our own gaze.

Thus said, within our practice, it is important not to dismiss the inherent complexity of reality by falsely presenting a closed answer to whatever problem we are called to address. This means that we believe that when confronted with a project, the process by which it will come to life is as important as the design stage. And that is part of the activity of being an architect. So, of course we are not immune to what happens in a global or local scale, but we are part of it and we react to it. Architecture, as said, produces culture but it is also determined by it. The changes mentioned have influenced or have affected us, for example, in the redesign of the working process. One good example is the current projects we have, which are not, directly, financed by those for whom we work. We are often confronted with a case where the client cannot pay for our services, so we need to look for ways of funding it, whether it be by public programs that can support us or by other means. This strategy comes from the belief that architecture must be present as the people's right to a better built environment. Architecture must strongly refuse to be used as a postcard where objects are presented

Community Kitchen of Terras da Costa, Photo FG+SG

as if they were some kind of autonomous entities that deserve to be contemplated. Our practice is situated outside of that logic. Architecture must respond to the demands of the times where it is being produced but also it must question the impositions it faces for its means of production.

When we are referring to context we are not only referring to physical or environmental aspects but also to society and to common issues—such as politics, economics, or philosophy—and individual issues that come from who is producing architecture. On the other hand, architecture requires that its producer is always updated, always reading what is happening around so that its production is more accurate and conscious. Don't forget doctors kill their biggest mistakes; architects give them life. That is a characteristic of all the intellectual professions, such as architecture.

Can you describe the meaning/understanding of "context" in your work and the ways this is manifested in your projects?

For us, the word "context" implies more than considering the simple physical and/or environmental site where the project is implemented.

We started in 2005 and began to participate in competitions—mainly public ones as many other conventional new offices in Portugal do. In 2008, with the economic crisis, all public works we had underway stopped, and we soon realized that a significant part of the population, despite their lack of means to hire our services and skills to build, did need architecture. This new reality was the trigger to start developing projects under the idea of working with the 99%. The method was very simple: identify needs and stakeholders in areas/neighborhoods that were in need of our services, collectively build a program, and start applying for funding. It was this new political and economic context that changed part of what is our practice. Of course, we continue to do traditional procurement. What we find challenging is to work in both ways and use architecture as a tool for social transformation.

That is why, for us, context is more than anything else the conditions—social, political, cultural, or all simultaneously—that are present in every project. What we say is that we neither agree with it being strictly linked with the site nor with the famous Koolhaas sentence of "fuck context" as a way to reclaim architecture´s autonomy regardless of the site. On the contrary, if the first is, naturally, important, it is only when complemented with the understanding of the means of production and the broader reality of where it is to be situated that a project can be sufficiently grounded, and better respond to the program.

Could you reflect on the ways such changes and transformations may facilitate new forms of architectural practices, collaborations, and multidisciplinary approaches?

We are not sure if it has always been the case but we presently feel that architecture is a practice that results from collective work, instead of being the result of an isolated inspired mind. New technologies, or a more complex reality of construction, for example, require the participation of different expertise. According to that, we have recently integrated a landscape architect and an anthropologist in our permanent team. It is not the first time that we collaborate with such disciplines in very concrete projects. The difference was that we felt the need for them to be part of our architecture production as a whole and not simply on specific projects where, perhaps, their presence would be more evident.

Presently, even though there is a continuity of the architect as a prominent figure—often a male, dressed in black and white or with bold hair—corresponding to a clear social class division that does not represent the actual production of our discipline, new forms of collectiveness have emerged that organize under a common and generic name. In what ways this new form will represent a permanent change is something we will have to wait to see. A cross-disciplinary way of collective work is for us the most interesting; however, that does not mean we argue in favor of a liquid reality where disciplines dilute and everyone can play all the roles. We believe in quite the

opposite; that each discipline has its own tools, and it is important to respect this as it is by the congregation of each different
gaze that the value of the responses we produce can be higher, or
more precise. At the end of the day, what comes out of our office
is architecture. What we mean is that the means of producing can
be different. Our discipline can be practiced without the need to
result in a constructed/built object but rather, as a way to question
and understand our present condition as a collective practice. Two
examples: OMA/AMO theoretical works that do not implicate the
construction but that feed their production by raising questions; or
the work of Forensic Architecture that, perhaps in a more practical
fashion, places architecture tools in the service of a political agenda,
directly questioning, for example, the ways in which territory is
used and manipulated or war is being made.

As said in the beginning, it is not clear that work in a collective way
is necessarily a novelty in architecture. Perhaps what is new is the
assumption that this path produces change in disassembling the
image that architecture is the discipline from which iconic buildings are produced. The absence of the need to build amplifies the
field of work and helps in the recognition that architecture is an
intellectual activity. This step closes the door to the often-absurd
discussion of what architecture really is and what it is not, and
opens up the possibility of placing architecture and the architects,
through social and political engagement, in direct connection with
broader issues where architecture has a say.

**Approaches to social projects with participatory design have
been prominent in recent years. Can you reflect on this?**

Some years ago we were ironically characterized as architects playing
sociologists. So, it is funny to now see so many architects reclaiming
that they practice a socially inspired architecture. Not only were we not,
and are not, playing the sociologist, as we reject the naming of "social
architecture" as a brand. What our discipline produces is inscribed in
the time and space in which we live, meaning, it has social impact. In
other words, we reject the idea of a non-social or asocial architecture.

The same goes with the term "participation." This concept—that seemed to have appeared from the outside, namely from political representatives as ways to build bottom-up processes of decision-making—is inherent to our practice; and by "our" we mean the discipline. Let's consider a more conventional program: the design of a family house. Aren't we suppose to question and interact with our client to understand their needs, dreams, etc. before and during the design process?

We are not playing naive here. Of course, at different scales participation acquires other forms and needs that need to be addressed differently. What we mean is that if we argue for architecture's role in transforming people's lives and their agency in defining the terms and conditions of our collective built environment, participation is a fundamental tool. The conditions and roles each one plays in participatory processes can be left open for definition according to each situation. If it is important to define each one's role but, at the end of the day, architecture is a public service, even when commissioned by private bodies.

Both terms, "social responsibility" and "participation," are as we argue, inherent to our discipline. Our challenge is to make it visible and evident through our practice. This means architecture must dispute those terms.

Can you tell us about any projects related to housing that you are currently working on? What is your ultimate goal when it comes to your work? How do global driving forces and local realities influence the design of houses? From your experience can you identify themes/issues/needs that appear constant in the design of houses and on the contrary others that need to change and adapt? Please present a case study.

First one needs to define what is meant by the term "house." For us, when considering housing projects, two scales are in conjunction: its domestic/interior and the relations between the different spaces that are contained within this unit; and, on the other hand,

Tanto Mar Exhibition,
Photo FG+SG

the relationship between units and with outside, the site where it is implemented. Both need to be considered simultaneously.

For the moment, even if we are developing several projects on housing, the most challenging one is our participation in the discussion to produce the first Housing Law in Portugal. Housing, even if it is considered as a basic human right and inscribed in our Constitution since 1976, is still not properly defined and transformed into national law. We have been very active in participating in discussions held at the Portuguese National Parliament where we had the opportunity to argue in favor of some principals that, for us, are foundational when discussing this matter: the right to housing, the right to basic energy supply, the right to the city, and the right to the place. It is our understanding that all four should be fully assumed and properly defined. If the first one is already evident as a basic human right, the other three come from what is our political positioning and also from the questions our work, in different contexts, imposes on us. In the last two to three years, especially since the electricity company was privatized, a number of precarious settlements saw their illegal electric systems being dismantled by the police, often with an aggressive attitude towards the inhab-

itants of such areas. If is true that those systems were indeed illegal and often linked to public lighting, it is also true that for those people no other solution was even presented. The access to energy is as fundamental as the access to tap water. So, by contemplating the right to basic energy supply we are giving a signal that no one should ever be prevented from any basic right. Not only should the right apply to those living in more informal conditions, but it also applies to those in the so-called formal city; they should never be without electricity due to economic difficulties preventing them from paying their bills. It should be remembered that Portugal has some of the more expensive electricity rates in Europe.

As for the right to the city and the right to the place, they almost go hand in hand. If the right to the city means that we all have the right to citizenship and to be part of the broader community that encompasses that space, the right to the place establishes that no one should be expelled to peripheral territories. This is particularly important when we are facing rehousing processes, where communities in the centre are often displaced from their relations either with each other or with the outside; for example, kids and the abrupt rupture that being forced to move to another school represents. We need to find solutions of territorial continuity, of sewing the urban fabric properly. In other words, what we argue for, when we talk about the right to the city and the right to the place, is for preventing, if not making it impossible, to design socially and spatially segregated areas destined to give shelter to lower classes, augmenting prejudices and injustice.

Other issues imposed on us include gender issues and the rights of non-documented citizens and ethnic communities targeted by racism and exclusion. All of them are present, directly or indirectly, when we question the access to housing.

Still related with housing, we are currently also working in the search for models of cohousing and cooperatives together with systems of neighbors' associations as part of the development of those same models.

Alvega Canoeing Center,
Photo Francisco Nogueira

Ultimately, maybe our first goal is not to discuss the internal dispo-
sition of a house (although the domestic space is also a reflection of
ways of understanding intimacy and the relations with the other),
but to discuss the access to it as a right, a right that is not exhausted
in the unit but on what it represents in a broader scale.

MOS

Housing No. 7

Housing No. 7
Affordable Artist Housing,
Studios, and Maker Space

Location:
Washington, DC

Program:
Housing, Studios,
Maker Space

Size:
65,000 square feet

Located on an avenue at the border of Washington, DC, and Maryland, Housing No. 7 is a fifty-six unit, four-story (plus penthouse) residential building meant to provide local artists with affordable housing, studios, maker spaces, and retail outlets to present their work. It is bound at its rear yard by neighboring residences and on its sides by a street and public alley, a quiet context that stands in contrast to the heavily trafficked avenue running along its front. Workspaces are set within the more residential section of the property, away from heavy traffic, while retail spaces are set to face the avenue. The remaining exterior space is given over to three open courtyards—one at the property's corner, separating building from the avenue–side street intersection, and two others at center-lot, opening onto the ground-floor lobby communal space.

This public, open space at the building's center forms a resolutely social heart around which residential levels are concentrically structured, doing away with the dark, enclosed, nonsocial corridors common to affordable housing projects. These communal spaces mirror each other across both residential wings: the elevators and stair cores connecting levels for living with those for working; twinned interior courtyards, opening each residential wing's center to light and air; U-shaped corridors, symmetrically wrapping around these courtyards; and residential units tracing the building's outer limits. Upending an unfortunate reality of most affordable housing today—the lack of windows, natural light, and ventilation—all residences have eight-by-eight-foot windows that open to the exterior, with views onto the wider communal space Housing No. 7 seeks to construct and support.

MOS

Housing No. 8
Apan Housing Laboratory

Location:
Apan, Hidalgo, Mexico

Program:
Master Plan and Welcome/
Education Center

Size:
Nine acres (master plan),
12,500 square feet
(Welcome Center)

Housing No. 8

This Welcome Center serves as the administrative heart and entry point for a nine-acre master plan of low-income housing prototypes for Apan, Mexico. (Offering the potential for growth, the housing prototypes proposed by the thirty-two selected architects varyingly rethink fundamentals of spatial organization, rework labor and construction, or recast structure and material.) These prototype houses as well as circular planters for gardening, brick water towers for on-site water storage, and playgrounds for residents and the wider community are all informally arranged across the steeply sloped site, within a grove of trees. Permeable paving and local ground cover demonstrate easily replicable models for developing the surrounding terrain while maintaining biodiversity of the site and ensuring the success of on-site cultivation.

The 12,500-square-feet, ceramic brick Welcome Center sits at the top of this slope, open to the local context and offering a place to survey the housing development downslope through east- and west-facing corridors. Tasked with accepting large groups bused to the site, presenting all housing prototypes, educating students, and providing short-term workspace, the building includes offices, a reading room, gallery, café, multipurpose room, and workshop. Four interior courtyards separate these programs while allowing movement and views across/through the structure. These courtyards combine with five skylights, spanning the entire width of the interior, to provide ample ventilation and controlled light to programmed spaces. The entire structure is topped with an accessible green roof, on which visitors can circulate around cubic courtyards and cylindrical skylights while viewing the surrounding context.

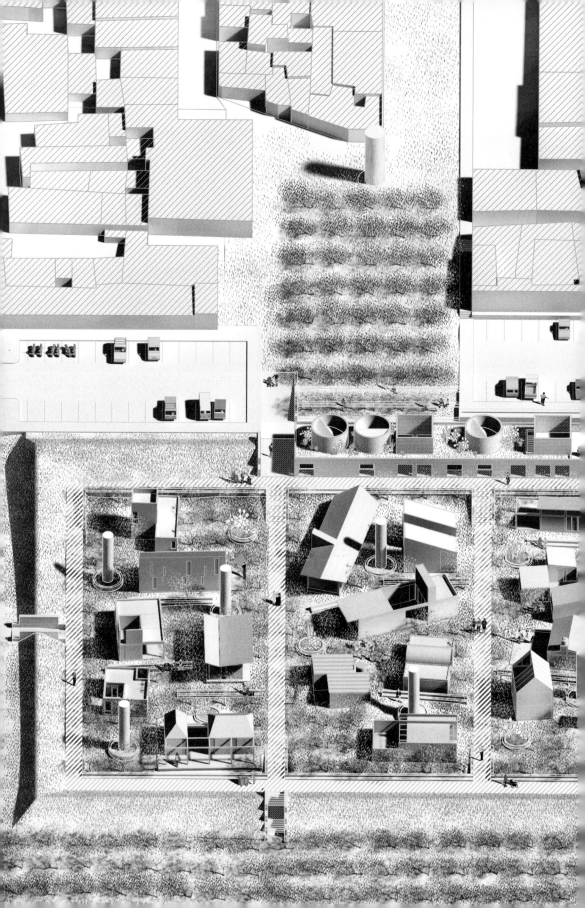

MOS

Tower No. 2

Location:
Saltillo, Mexico

Program:
Housing, Retail

Size:
400 square meters

Tower No. 2

Tower No. 2 (currently untitled) is a mixed-use project in Saltillo, Mexico. The building is a concrete framework that contains one courtyard, one ground-floor retail space, two staircases (one shared and one private, intertwined), two roof terraces (one shared and one private, separated), and four duplex units. Units No. 1 and No. 3 face a rear yard and wrap the courtyard with private hallways, stairs, and balconies; units No. 2 and No. 4 front the main street. All residences include a living area, kitchen, storage space, and laundry on their public first level, as well as two bedrooms, one bathroom, and additional storage on a second level.

Urban Nouveau   Incremental India

"We look at the journey and growth of an idea that shapes into a project, and then into a studio practice, trying to understand what everyday lives and urban dreams are made of, and developing a strategy that integrates private lives and city ecosystems. The idea of incremental housing development is something that needs attention as cities are being forced to undergo drastic changes under the banner of cluster development that wipes out the nature and structure of living that already exists often with much merit and experiences."

Filipe Balestra, Urban Nouveau

The birth of Urban Nouveau took place in India during the realization of their first project, Incremental India. The project was the culmination of a series of initiatives that Filip Balestra and Sara Goranson had already undertaken in Rocinha, one of the largest favelas in Rio de Janeiro. Rocinha "little farm" used to be a farm with banana and mango trees, but it was transformed into homes for somewhere between 250,000 and 350,000 people. The project was developed in close collaboration with the community and included the construction of social housing, a school, and a social center.

The architects were deeply concerned with the fact that in spite of great progress in improving slums and preventing their formation, the slum challenge remained a critical factor for the persistence of poverty in the world, excluding fellow humans from the benefits of urbanization and from fair and equal opportunities to attain individual and collective progress (UN-Habitat 2015). According to UN-Habitat, approximately thirty-three percent, 863 million people, of the urban population in the developing world in 2012 lived in slums.

"… something that is very interesting is to understand that about 40 to 50 per cent of all urbanity is slum land, and most of us architects are working for the rich when we could be working for the poor. Say, what if, instead of building one house that costs 1 million, we could build 100,000 houses that cost 10,000 each? Perhaps we can widen up the angle of how we look into our cities, into their architecture and most specifically, into our business."

Filipe Balestra, Urban Nouveau

These concerns fueled the architects' interest in proposing affordable social housing, developed in close collaboration with the existing inhabitants. The project took place in Yerawada, Pune, an urban village close to Koregaon Park in the south and the Gandhi Memorial on a mountain in the north. Great controversies are observed in this area, where one can find a golf course with 24/7 water supply in close proximity, as opposed to the local population of the underprivileged Yerawada, who receive water once or twice in the middle of the night. Furthermore, the project had to be realized with a very limited budget since the average governmental budget for social housing had been significantly reduced. Despite the fact that the whole process was fraught with difficulties, it was underpinned by valuable insights, tools, and methodologies in addressing inequalities, exclusion, and lack of accessibility to basic housing needs.

Learning from Local Collaborations. The architects collaborated closely with local social groups, professionals, and the informal workforce in an attempt to gain a deeper insight into the local sociospatial realities. They thus acquired a more nuanced understanding of the opportunities and challenges presented by the local political, ethical, and social particularities. A local group, Mahila Milan, controls the local community through what the architects called a parallel tax system. The group is responsible for the community's savings through the collection of money from the families in order to invest them into projects that will improve their infrastructure and living conditions (schools, nurseries, houses). The leader of Mahila Milan introduced the architects to the local population, explained their intentions, and facilitated a close collaboration based on mutual trust and understanding. During the construction phase the architects worked on site, together with Guilherme Lima, the chief local builder.

Learning from the Context. The team went through an awareness phase, conducting close observation through and across scales—the existing housing units, the neighborhoods, the site conditions in the whole village, as well as the surrounding, wider context that had an impact on the village—*"to create a collective understanding of how it works. This means before designing architecture, let's zoom out, let's look at the context, let's taste it, let's listen and let's understand what's really going on."*

In an attempt to understand the local context on both rational and emotional levels, detailed measurement and mapping of the spatial layouts of the existing houses and neighborhoods were performed as well as a mapping of the daily activities and practices of the inhabitants. (We measured the space in between houses and mapped the activities that were going on during our presence in the place.) So, to fractal and organic urban fabrics, which is very interesting—no street is the same, no house is the same. Even though people are dealing with industrialized components, every house is unique. There is no design repetition.

The detailed field study revealed a complex urban ecosystem that emerged from the houses' financial situation and the local way of living. Materials and food were used to their full potential; for example, the leftovers from the cooking of vegetables were used as food for their animals on a daily basis; the kitchen was transformed through the day, from the place where women performed their everyday rituals to a socializing space with the neighbors; the narrow walkways were used as passages during the day and transformed into shared spaces, "meeting rooms" where women would wash their vessels, meet, and socialize in the mornings.

"Being on site every day, listening and understanding, one quickly realizes" the existence of two types of houses in these villages: the kaccha and the pukka house. Kaccha is the name given to the temporary house that has been temporary for probably twenty, thirty or forty years; and pukka is name given to the house of a family that either got lucky in business or of a charismatic, talented businessman who creates a well-built house in his village. Due to the limited budget, the team decided that the project should focus on the kaccha house, as these inhabitants were in a greater need of their service. The kaccha houses are organized into singles, doubles, triples, quadruples, and even larger clusters. Furthermore, the typology "Shop Plus One," the name given by the company to the double-story family houses where local families live on the first floor and sell their products on the ground floor in order to earn a living, was also proposed.

Learning through the design phase. A significant aspect of the design process was the continuous communication between the architects and the local community from the very initial stages, when the locals expressed their needs, dreams, and aspirations. During this phase, community leaders provided feedback for the prototypes proposed by the team, offering further insights into the locals' tendencies of space appropriation as well as their everyday patterns of living.

Furthermore, the project strategically proposed the actual engagement of the local community in the realization process in order to reduce the cost; each beneficiary family would give a contribution of 10 percent. However, since for many families this kind of contribution was impossible, the strategy featured a possibility for a sweat contribution in which each family would help demolishing the old shack and rebuilding the new house.

Jawaharlal Nehru National Urban Renewal Mission

The JNNURM was launched in 2005 as the first flagship scheme of the Indian Ministry. JNURM implemented by MoHUPA has two components, Basic Services for Urban poor (BSUP) and Integrated Housing and Slum Development Programme (IHSDP), which aims at integrated development of slums through projects for providing shelter, basic services, and other related civic amenities with a view to providing utilities to the urban poor.

The two components of JNNURM were mandated to pursue three key pro-poor reforms, namely (a) earmarking of twenty-five percent of the municipal budget for provision of basic services including affordable housing to the urban poor; (b) implementation of the Seven-Point Charter, namely provision of land tenure, affordable housing, water, sanitation, education, health and social security to the poor in a time-bound manner ensuring convergence with other programs; and (c) reservation of twenty-five percent of developed land in all housing projects, public or private, critical for slum improvement.

Three housing prototypes were developed:

House A: a basic two-level home that is structured to receive an additional floor above without bringing the risk of structural hazard.

House B: a similar typology to House A but it is on stilts. The aim was to provide a "Shop Plus One" structure, although due to the fact the government would not invest housing revenue in a privately owned shop the ground floor was left free for "customization." To support the function of a shop, a roller shutter door was installed, allowing it to be used also as a rickshaw park. The fact that the home is on the first floor, renders it suitable to be placed in valleys, where the monsoon waters accumulate to a high level, threatening to destroy a house's electrics.

House C: a typology between House A and House B.

Learning from Chilean architect Alejandro Aravena's practice, the team attempted to provide one-third more space to each family, since maximum areas for these kinds of projects are always super small. The strategy also aimed at bringing infrastructures such as water, waste-water removal, and electricity into every home.

Four years since the initial field study and the design of the three prototypes, one thousand houses are under construction. More information about this project can be found at: *http://mohua.gov.in/cms/jawaharlal-nehru-national-urban-renewal-mission.php (JNNURM & BSUP: Jawaharlal Nehru National Urban Renewal Mission & Basic Services for Urban Poor).*

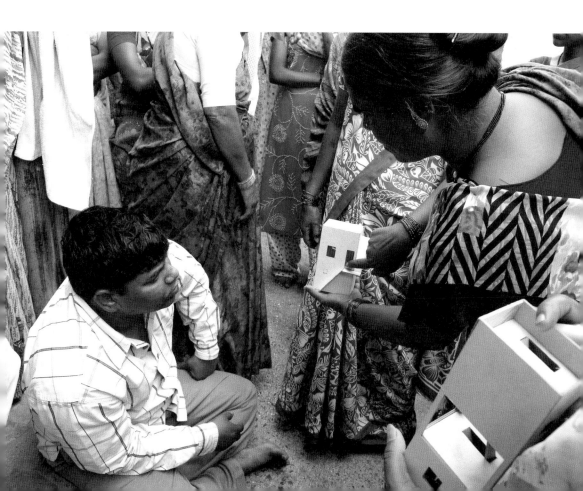

Shigeru Ban

The Humanitarian Works of Shigeru Ban

1 Bruderlein, C., Jacobson, H. Z., Ban, S. (2014). Shigeru Ban. Humanitarian Architecture.

Shigeru Ban is well known for his humanitarian approach to design, in an attempt to respond to the needs of displaced populations as a result of natural disasters. This particular work addresses timely challenges faced by contemporary architects such as the absence of the traditional client; and the need for social entrepreneurship, social responsibility, a nuanced understanding of the local context and the people's cultural and social makeup, and the sustainability of the shelters. For the past three decades, Shigeru Ban has applied his extensive knowledge of recyclable, inexpensive local materials, particularly paper and cardboard, to construct high-quality, low-cost shelters for victims of disaster across the world, training and involving local resources and labor. The presented work is part of the disaster relief projects that the office has undertaken in the past few years, with a focus on elemental dwellings/shelters which have managed to restore *"comfort, protection, dignity, and daily routine to uprooted refugees."* [1]

For the realization of the projects a wide network of different actors and stakeholders (both local and international) participate in the process. These include donors (both of money and of contributions such as sheets for surfaces and tents), transportation companies, prefabrication construction companies, and volunteers helping construct the shelters.

To date, Shigeru Ban has developed several types of emergency shelters using paper tubes as structural elements and beer cases as foundations. In projects such as in Rwanda (2004), Haiti (2010), and Nepal (2015), the same structural elements were implemented in the realization of the emergency shelters. Paper tubes were considered a cheap and easy way to find material in any country. In each case though, adjustments were made regarding the material of the connectors based on the availability of local materials. According to the architects there are three questions that are considered in

Kirinda House Post-Tsuna-mi Rehabilitation Project

Location:
Kirinda, Hambantota,
Sri Lanka

Building Area:
71 square meters/house

Total Floor Area:
71 square meters/house

Structure:
One Story, compressed earth blocks

Finishing Materials:
Timber and compressed earth blocks

Construction Dates:
2005–06

terms of temporary housing: Firstly, what will it be in the future? Secondly, will it be rubbish? And lastly, will it be a permanent residence that is unsuitable within the local landscape?

The paper log house can be assembled by anyone and then paper tubes and beer cases can be recycled in order to avoid any problems of industrial waste. Anyone who participates in the construction of a paper log house in that situation could not find themselves spiritually untouched. Moreover, it is different to construct temporary housing with one's own labor than it is to simply purchase ready-made accommodation. Even if the paper log houses themselves were pulled down after the years, the paper log house will remain in the minds of the people who built and lived in them. In the future, our activity will progress to a next step, by cooperating with residents and by improving the quality of pre-fabricated kits.

Tsunami Reconstruction Project—Sri Lanka, 2007
Located in the southeast coast of Sri Lanka, Kirinda is an Islamic village of fishermen. Most of the village's buildings were swept away during the catastrophic tsunami on December 26, 2004. The villagers were forced to live in temporary houses under severe conditions. This post-tsunami rehabilitation project includes the construction of sixty-seven houses and a mosque and tree planting.

Each house has two bedrooms, a hall, and a roofed courtyard, which is a semi-open space. The hall and the roofed courtyard could be a large room, a space that had an important role in the life of the inhabitants, where they could have a meal with family, enjoy socializing with neighbors and repair their fishing nets and equipment. An important part of the design process was thus, the adjustment of the house to its context. The house was spatially organized in accordance to the locals' cultural and social specificities as well as adapted to the environmental and weather conditions of the area. Additionally, local, low-cost materials that could be used to build houses in a short time were chosen for its construction. Since this is a rehabilitation project, it was important that it was low budget and had a short construction period. The principal material is CEB

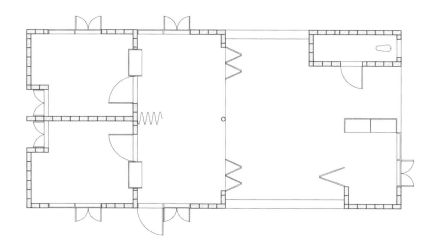

(compressed earth block), which is available in Sri Lanka at a low cost and doesn't need builders. The block has un uneven surface so that it can be easily interlocked and built up like LEGO.

Paper Temporary Shelter—Philippines 2013
This is the temporary shelter constructed at Daanbantayan, Cebu, Philippines, following the devastation of Typhoon Haiyan (locally called Yolanda) in November of 2013. The construction methods of previous paper log house projects (in Japan, Turkey, and India) were very complicated and time-consuming to build in high volumes. In this design, we have incorporated the Paper Partition connection system (developed for making partitions within evacuation centers), which made it possible to simplify the construction, thus shortening the construction period. The foundations were made from beer crates filled with sand bags, and floor panels were made from coconut wood and plywood. A readily used woven bamboo sheet was applied to the paper tube structural frame, and the roof is a thatching of Nypa palms laid over plastic sheets. The construction was carried out in cooperation with students from the University of San Carlos in Cebu.

Container Temporary Housing—Japan, 2011
Since the 2011 earthquake in Japan, we have visited more than fifty evacuation facilities and installed over 1,800 units (two by two meters) of our Paper Partition System to ensure privacy between families. During that time, I heard the news that the town of Onagawa was having difficulty constructing enough temporary housing due to the insufficient amount of flat land. Therefore, we decided to propose three-story temporary housing made from shipping containers. By stacking these containers in a checkerboard pattern, our system creates bright, open living spaces in between the containers. The standard temporary houses issued by the government are poorly made, and there is not enough storage space. We installed built-in closets and shelves in all of our houses with the help of volunteers and with the donation fund. It has become a breakthrough and precedent to new government standards of evacuation facilities and temporary housing.

Paper Log House Turkey

Paper Temporary Shelters—Nepal 2015

On the 25th of April 2015, Nepal suffered a 7.8-magnitude earthquake. Because of the office's continuous involvement in disaster relief projects around the world over the last twenty years, several requests for support were received. Discussions with the local community in order to express their needs, both physical and emotional, guided the design choices and processes; the knowledge of the local population renders them suitable for their involvement in both the preparation and realization stages of the project. Research on the local houses, in terms of construction materials and methods, provided inspiration and informed ideas that were implemented on the constructed shelters. A workshop with local stakeholders, Nepalese graduates, and students was arranged and a paper tube construction (using duct tape to secure paper tube joints for the first time) was proposed. A wall system that can be

assembled by connecting modular wooden frames (90 centimeters × 210 centimeters) and infilling with rubbled bricks was proposed. This simple construction method enables anyone to assemble the wooden frames very quickly; and if a roof (a truss made of local paper tubes) is secured on top, and the wooden structure is covered with a plastic sheet, people can immediately begin to inhabit the shelters. Afterwards, people can stack the rubbled bricks inside the wooden frames and slowly complete the construction themselves.

Paper Log House—India, 2001

Paper Log House India (right)
Photo Kartikeya Shodhan
Paper Shelter Philippines (left)

What makes the India log house unique is the foundation and the roof. Rubble from destroyed building was used for the foundation instead of beer crates, which could not be found in this area. It was coated with a traditional mud floor. For the roof, split bamboo was applied to the rib vaults and whole bamboo to the ridge beams. A

locally woven cane mat was placed over the bamboo ribs, followed by a clear plastic tarpaulin to protect against rain, then another cane mat. Ventilation was provided through the gables, where small holes in the mats allowed air to circulate. This ventilation also allowed cooking to be done inside, with the added benefit of repelling mosquitoes.

UN-Habitat
Lebanon

Empowering People:
Socially Engaged Design

The project presented describes the process of implementing a safe, inclusive, and accessible public space in Naba'a, a low-income neighborhood in eastern Beirut, through the participation and training of the local community. A quick field assessment was conducted in coordination with Bourj Hammoud municipality and key stakeholders in Naba'a to identify a potential space to implement the project. Many vacant areas were identified but most of them were private. The only available vacant space was an area measuring 200 square meters owned by the municipality, located within a residential area in the heart of Naba'a. A formal approval was granted by Bourj Hammoud municipality in order to implement a public space design on this property. This space however was being used as a coffee shop known to be a hub for drug users. Therefore the first intervention in coordination with the municipality as well as the local committee was to remove the coffee shop from the site. The following steps were carried out as pre-preparation for the intervention:

1. Creation of a local committee: As the UN-Habitat aims to engage the community in all phases of the project, a local committee of fourteen people was established in Naba'a including key stakeholders and community leaders, such as Mokhtars, school directors, civil activists, representatives of active political parties as well as a representative from Bourj Hammoud municipality. The main objective behind the creation of this committee was to ensure that the main needs of the community were assessed and met in the design of the project as well as to ensure project's ownership and sustainability.

2. Development of a Minecraft Model: The participatory design of the Naba'a public space was developed with the help of Minecraft Model, an innovative tool previously used by UN-Habitat in several countries but for the first time in Lebanon. A technical study was prepared by the responsible engineer from UN-Habitat in order to collect all needed information about the site. A set of materials

was collected, including photographs, Google maps and images, and GIS maps. The materials were then shared with the Minecraft modelers in order to start creation of the model which took around four weeks before the final validation.

3. Conducting orientation sessions: prior to the Minecraft workshop, multiple orientation sessions were conducted with the community. The targeted groups were as follows: children from five to twelve years of age; adolescents from twelve to eighteen years old; youth from eighteen to twenty-five years old; women over twenty-five years of age; and men over twenty-five years old. The selection of participants took into consideration gender aspects, the presence of Syrian refugees, and the inclusion of persons with disabilities. The orientation sessions aimed to introduce the project, provided basic awareness on public spaces (what is public space, typologies of public spaces, why public spaces are important, the benefits of public spaces, etc.), defined the main problems of the space, and selected the participants for the Minecraft Workshop. The main highlighted problems of the space were related to safety and security, the presence of drug users, the small size of the space, and the space users (is it only for children, for youth, or for the whole family?; is it for Lebanese or Syrians?). Around 120 persons from all age groups living within the geographical spectrum of the space participated in these orientation sessions.

Civil works began in March 2017 involving local workers who were hired by the contractor. The 200-square-meter area was covered with three distinct types of surfaces. The entrance and the surrounding sidewalk of the site were repaired using interlocking tiles with no mortar so that the water infiltrates and seeps into the green grass area (storm water reuse). Additionally, the sidewalk became more user-friendly as it is now accessible for individuals with physical disabilities. The site itself was divided into three zones` with play-friendly, soft surfaces—in the middle lies a green lawn with grey rubber surfaces on each side. Two steel tents were installed above parts of each of the rubber sections to provide shade and shelter from the rain and a resting area for parents escorting their kids to the space. Under the larger steel tent, concrete benches and picnic tables were arranged. In addition, a water tank was installed on the roof of the tent to irrigate the vegetation on site using the neighboring building's water overflow. A gutter that collects rain water and discharges it under the grass was also added.

On the August 3, 2017, UN-Habitat Lebanon organized in collaboration with the local committee and the municipality of Bourj Hammoud an inauguration ceremony of the Naba'a public space. The event was funded by the Norwegian Ministry of Foreign Affairs and the Italian Cooperation, and comprised short speeches by the stakeholders, ribbon cutting, as well as animated activities for children. Shortly before six in the evening, the starting time of the ceremony, the streets were packed with individuals of all ages; Lebanese, Syrian, and other nationalities, women, men, and children. The street was closed to cars during the afternoon and local vendors installed temporary kiosks selling food and beverages. Entertainment for the children was provided by mime artists and clowns from the neighborhood.

Biographies

Nadia Charalambous trained as an architect and has been working as an academic and researcher at the University of Cyprus since 2008. She studied architecture at the Bartlett School of Architecture, University College London, University of London where she received her BSc, MSc in Advanced Architectural Studies and the Diploma in Architecture. She subsequently completed her Ph.D. studies at NTUA, Athens. Underpinning all research and professional activities is a continuous interest in the sociospatial dimensions of society and culture through a combination of spatial and social research methods.

Giorgos Kyriazis is an architect, adjunct professor, researcher, and PhD candidate at the University of Cyprus where he has been teaching architectural design studio, supervising Diploma students, and curating exhibitions. His research interest focuses on the role of image in our constructed imaginary and its subsequent effects on the architectural production. He graduated with honors in excellence in design, research proposal award, and portfolio honorarium from Columbia University Masters program. His practice is based on a multidisciplinary approach that involves projects varying from architecture to graphic design as well as tutoring workshops throughout Europe. In 2012 he was one of the representatives of the Cyprus Pavilion, Revisit—Customizing Tourism, at the Venice Biennale.

Urban Nouveau
Sara Göransson is an architect, building engineer, and founding partner of the international award-winning agency Urban Nouveau. Having attained the Andrew Grant Progress Award during her bachelors of architecture at the Edinburgh Collage of Art, Sara pursued her interests and trained with VMX in Amsterdam before completing her masters degree at the Royal Institute of Technology in Stockholm.

Filipe Balestra is an holistic designer, urban developer, and founding partner of Urban Nouveau. Balestra trained at the Edinburgh College of Art and at Royal Institute of Technology in Stockholm and worked for Rem Koolhaas/OMA where he realized projects including the Hermitage Museum extension in Saint Petersburg and the Jeddah Airport in Saudi Arabia.

Current projects include the implementation of Connecting-Stockholm which led Urban Nouveau to become advisors to the Government of Japan and to the Government of Malaysia, as well as the construction of 1,000 houses for the urban poor in the slums of India and a proposal for the future development of 7 villages in Upplands-Väsby, Sweden.

MOS
Michael Meredith and Hilary Sample are American architects and cofounders of the award-winning architecture firm MOS Architects in New York City. Michael Meredith received a masters of architecture from the Harvard Graduate School of Design. Hilary Sample graduated with a masters in architecture from Princeton. Meredith and Sample teach at Princeton University School of Architecture and Columbia University, respectively,

and their academic research occurs in parallel to the real-world constraints of practice, informing both. Recent projects include four studio buildings for the Krabbesholm Højskole campus, the Museum of Outdoor Arts Element House visitor center, the Floating House on Lake Huron, and the Lali Gurans Orphanage and Learning Center in Kathmandu, Nepal.

Ateliermob. Tiago Mota Saraiva is an architect, urban planner and managing partner at ateliermob and director of the co-op Working with the 99%. He holds a degree in architecture and a postgraduate diploma in Architecture, Territory, and Memory. He was an invited assistant professor at the Universidade Moderna and at the Faculty of Architecture at the University of Lisbon. He has been an effective member of the National Board of the Association of Architects, and was a member of the Executive Board of the Portuguese Association of Architects 03/07 and National Treasurer 05/07. In addition, Tiago Mota Saraiva was a member of the Organizing Committee of the Portuguese National Architecture Year, 03. He writes a weekly opinion column on the Portuguese national daily *i* and monthly *dia 15*. He is a board member of the socio-cultural co-op Largo Residências and of the European Re:Kreators Association and he is member of the editorial board of *Le Monde Diplomatique - Portuguese Version*.

UN-Habitat Lebanon was initiated in late 2006. As the country has faced two large scale crises—the July 2006 War on Lebanon, and the Syrian Refugee Crisis—the program steered most of its activities to focus on responding to emerging issues through housing reconstruction, shelter provision, and basic services upgrading while also laying the foundation for long-term sustainable solutions. The projects of UN-Habitat in Lebanon are aligned along specific key focus areas, such as housing and urban design.

Shigeru Ban was born in Tokyo in 1957. He graduated from the Cooper Union and started working for Arata Isozaki & Associates in 1982. He founded Shigeru Ban Architects in 1985 and became consultant to the United Nations High Commissioner for Refugees (UNHCR) in 1995. He established the NGO, Voluntary Architects' Network (VAN) in the same year to support disaster relief. Selected works include Nicolas G. Hayek Center, Centre Pompidou-Metz, and Oita Prefecture Art Museum. He is the recipient of multiple awards, including Grande Médaille d'or de l'Académie d'architecture (2004), Arnold W. Brunner Memorial Prize in Architecture (2005), Grand Prize of AIJ (2009), Honorary Doctorate from Technische Universität München (2009), L'Ordre des Arts et des Lettres, France (legrade d'offcier) (2010), Auguste Perret Prize (2011), Art Prize from the Japanese Agency for Cultural Affairs (2012), L'Ordre des Arts et des Lettres, France (le grade de commandeur) (2014), JIA Gran Prix (2016), and Mother Teresa Social Justice Award (2017). He served as professor at Keio University (2001–08), Visiting Professor of Harvard University GSD and Cornell University (2010), and currently Professor at Kyoto University of Art and Design (from 2011), guest professor at Keio University (from 2015). He was Laureate of the 2014 Pritzker Architecture Prize.

Publication Credits

Writers
Nadia Charalambous
Giorgos Kyriazis

Contributors
Ateliermob, MOS
Urban Nouveau
Shigeru Ban
UN-Habitat Lebanon

Students
Anastasia Psoma
Aristofanis H'charalambous
Andreas Konstantinou
Andronikos Kalli
Christos Dionysis
Christos Georgiou
Irini Klidara
Kateryna Chrysostomou
Lefteris Kaimakliotis
Michalis Psara
Mikaella Raspa
Nasia Pantelidou
Paisios Skitini
Savvas Dimitriou
Stefanos Kyprianou

Book Design
Giorgos Kyriazis

Cover
Giorgos Kyriazis, Anastasia Psoma, Aristofanis H'charalambous, Michalis Psara

Proofreading
Christen Jamar

Design and setting
Giorgos Kyriazis

Lithography
Giorgos Kyriazis

Printed in the European Union

Bibliographic information published by the Deutsche Nationalbibliothek
The Deutsche Nationalbibliothek lists this publication in the Deutsche Nationalbibliografie; detailed bibliographic data are available on the Internet at http://dnb.d-nb.de

jovis Verlag GmbH
Kurfürstenstraße 15/16
10785 Berlin

www.jovis.de

jovis books are available worldwide in select bookstores. Please contact your nearest bookseller or visit www.jovis.de for information concerning your local distribution.

ISBN 978-3-86859-523-9